OPTIMISM
PRESS

Trust First

Trust First

*A True Story About the Power
of Giving People Second Chances*

BRUCE DEEL

with SARA GRACE

OPTIMISM PRESS

OPTIMISM PRESS
An imprint of Penguin Random House LLC
penguinrandomhouse.com

Most Optimism Press books are available at a discount when purchased in quantity for
sales promotions or corporate use. Special editions, which include personalized covers,
excerpts, and corporate imprints, can be created when purchased in large quantities. For
more information, please call (212) 572-2232 or e-mail specialmarkets@penguinrandom
house.com. Your local bookstore can also assist with discounted bulk purchases using
the Penguin Random House corporate Business-to-Business program. For assistance in
locating a participating retailer, e-mail B2B@penguinrandomhouse.com.

Library of Congress Cataloging-in-Publication Data

Names: Deel, Bruce, author. | Grace, Sara, author.
Title: Trust first : a true story about the power of giving people
second chances / Bruce Deel with Sara Grace.
Description: New York : Optimism Press, [2019] | Description based on print version
record and CIP data provided by publisher; resource not viewed.
Identifiers: LCCN 2019002109 (print) | LCCN 2019004723 (ebook) |
ISBN 9780525538189 () | ISBN 9780525538172 (hardcover)
Subjects: LCSH: City of Refuge (Nonprofit organization) | Poor--Services
for--Georgia--Atlanta. | Church work with the poor--Georgia--Atlanta. |
Community development--Georgia--Atlanta.
Classification: LCC HV99.A72 (ebook) | LCC HV99.A72 C5834 2019 (print) |
DDC 362.5/57509758231--dc23
LC record available at https://lccn.loc.gov/2019002109

Printed in the United States of America
1   3   5   7   9   10   8   6   4   2

Book design by Gretchen Achilles

Dedicated to the memory of Rev. Cecil B. Deel,

my giant of a father

Contents

SECTION THREE

A Letter from Simon Sinek

The vision is clear: to build a world in which the vast majority of people wake up every single morning inspired, feel safe at work, and return home fulfilled at the end of the day. I believe the best way to build this world is with leaders. Good leaders. Great leaders. And so, I've devoted my professional life to help find, build, and support the leaders who are committed to leading in a way that will more likely bring that vision to life.

Unfortunately, the practice of leadership is so misunderstood. It has nothing to do with rank. It has nothing to do with authority. Those things may come with a leadership position and they may help a leader operate with greater efficiency and at greater scale, but those things do not a leader make. Leadership is not about being in charge, it's about taking care of those in our charge. It is about creating an environment in which people can rise to their natural best. It is a distinctly human endeavor. None of us is an expert in leadership. The practice of leadership is a journey and we are all students. It is therefore our collective responsibility to share the lessons, tools, and ideas that are helping each of us to become the leaders we wish we had so that others may benefit. *Trust First* is one of those ideas.

When I first heard Bruce Deel's story, I was left speechless. He has an ability to trust in a way that I have never seen before. He is willing to extend trust to people who most of society has deemed untrustworthy. Bruce and his wife let drug addicts into their home. They let prostitutes babysit his children. For any parent reading this, simply reading those words likely sends shivers down your spine. However, by learning to trusting first, Bruce has been able to help transform people's lives in ways few could have imagined.

This was the reason I wanted to share Bruce's story with as many people as possible. Though I do not expect many people to extend trust in the extreme way in which Bruce does, his story proves the transformative power of trust and how we can all do better at trusting the people in our lives.

Too many of us treat trust like a valuable asset that must be guarded. That we can give it away only after someone has proved themselves worthy. Bruce shatters that assumption. If we can all learn to take the risk to trust first, it gives those around us permission to believe in themselves and their abilities in the most remarkable way. And if people can learn to trust in themselves, they will also learn to trust others in a deeper way. The result of which helps build stronger, more powerful and, indeed, more trusting teams.

Enjoy Bruce's story for what it is: remarkable. And as you read, take notes on the underlying lessons we can all learn about the transformative power of trust.

Trust first and inspire on!

Simon Sinek

Section One

CHAPTER 1

A Gentle Downward Pressure

The aberration is not the good person.
It is the bad person. We are made for goodness.

—ARCHBISHOP DESMOND TUTU[*]

Twenty years ago, I showed up on a dilapidated corner of Bankhead Highway, in one of Atlanta's roughest corridors, with a van full of food. I had just formed a nonprofit called City of Refuge, and this was my first attempt to go out into the community to serve people in crisis, people who for whatever reason had not found a safe, comfortable path through the wilderness of life.

Maybe you'll be surprised to hear this, or maybe you won't: My first meal did not go smoothly. In fact, in the narrow window of three terrifying minutes, it made me wonder if I should go home and throw in the towel for good.

My first meal service was well underway that day, with a

[*] Dalai Lama, Desmond Tutu, Douglas Carlton Abrams, *The Book of Joy: Lasting Happiness in a Changing World* (New York: Penguin Random House, 2016), 267.

crowd of fifty or so people gathered for the best hot chili my wife Rhonda, a few volunteers, and I could put together. I was filling my umpteenth plastic bowl when I heard screaming. First a female voice, then a male one, in a jumbled string of obscenities. I scanned for the noise and saw a woman reach into her jacket pocket and pull out a gun.

My worries about what might go wrong that evening had been things like, *What if we run out of cheese? What if we can't plate food fast enough?* I hadn't once thought, *What if someone pulls out a .45-caliber pistol?* I was a white Christian pastor from rural Virginia who now lived in the Atlanta suburbs—in other words, an interloper with no real knowledge of the streets. Nevertheless, I had shown up believing I could do some good by serving a desperate need.

People nearby immediately scattered into shadows and around corners. I then had a clear line of sight to the object of this woman's fury: a rail-thin man in baggy, dirty sweatpants. His face showed hints of worn-away rouge and kohl that I wasn't sure what to make of. He was as aggressive as someone with a gun pointed in his face could possibly be, hurling insults that seemed to dare her to pull the trigger. Catcalls rang out from the shadows, excited fanfare that contrasted wildly with my own anxiety.

Over the next months, years, and eventually decades, I would come to know these two angry combatants intimately. But that day, I had no idea who they were or how they had arrived there. I didn't know if they knew each other. I didn't know whether the gun had bullets or if Gloria (a name I would learn later) had ever pulled the trigger before. I didn't know exactly why they were so angry, so volatile, so seemingly bent on destruction at just the moment when a hot meal was coming their way. I knew only that they were matching each other stare for stare, threat for threat. My breath caught in my throat as sweat beaded my brow.

I glanced back at the building behind me, an empty warehouse beside a liquor store. The one volunteer who had come with me that day was standing inside the building's storm door, holding the handle. I could tell by the look on his face that he was holding the door shut, unwilling to step out into the fray.

I didn't know yet that Gloria was seen on the streets as an unusually kind soul, a pleasant conversationalist who was known to share a blanket on a cold night or food from her own meager stash. I didn't know that she was alcoholic or how hard it was to combine that illness with being black and poor and come up with anything other than tragedy.

Though the whooping crowd had an obvious favorite (Gloria), I didn't know that Rufus was unanimously regarded as belligerent and hateful, quick to cut those with whom he disagreed, seemingly without reason. Nor did I know anything about his background—that he had never had a safe place where he was loved unconditionally and that the closest approximation he'd had was a community of needle-sharing prostitutes. I didn't know how many churches, erstwhile sanctuaries for those in need, had turned him away or imposed conditions for participation that Rufus was unwilling to comply with.

I also didn't know how poorly I understood poverty and the ways it traps and traumatizes those in its grasp. Like so many privileged people, I had considered the problems of the poor only through the filter of my own experience. I've already said I'm a white guy from Virginia. While my family didn't have much money and my childhood was less than conventional, I had the privilege of two loving parents with high expectations for my future and a home of security, love, and opportunity. In other words, I was born with momentum.

I didn't understand yet that poverty isn't caused by bad decisions as much as it compels them. I didn't recognize what I now call *opportunity injustice*, the individual and systemic factors that lock people in crisis—poverty, untreated mental illness, and addiction, and the criminalization of all three.

Of course, knowing all that wouldn't have been much help in a gunfight anyway. Something more instinctive took me over—call it adrenaline, or the stirrings of my upbringing. Growing up in the mountains of southwest Virginia, I was no stranger to a fight. I had never run from a conflict, and I didn't run from this one. Instead, I stepped gingerly between Gloria and Rufus, who at this point had both gone silent, furious eyes speaking loudly enough. I gently placed my hand on Gloria's. The steel barrel of the gun protruded from our coupled hands and she gave no indication of backing down.

"You don't really want to do this, do you?" I asked.

As I said the words, I put just the slightest bit of gentle downward pressure on her hand. Time seemed to hang for a moment, none of us sure what would come next. But then I felt the tension ease in Gloria's body like a sigh. She dropped her arm to her side and slipped the gun into her jacket pocket. Rufus continued his mouthy commentary as I shared a moment with Gloria, a deep sorrow in her eyes. She turned quickly and moved down the sidewalk, only her shadow walking with her. Rufus looked at the group that had enthusiastically booed him, taunted them with a smile, and turned to collect a bowl of chili from the table. I worked to slow my breathing, wiped the sweat from my face, and steadied myself against the table.

I finished the food service that day feeling exhausted and heavy of heart. I didn't want to have to go back to my family and tell them I might have put myself in harm's way. I didn't want to admit that the process of transformation I had imagined initiating that day with a kind word and a warm meal wasn't going to be very successful if every meal became a gunfight—or worse, if someone ended up wounded or dead on the street.

I had arrived that day believing that each and every person was worthy of my humble resources of food, time, and attention. The day's events hadn't changed that. The day had made me realize just how humble my contribution would be, at least at first, given how little I knew these people and their problems. Had I been stupid to think I could make a difference? Sure, they needed something or someone—but did they need *me*?

And then I thought about that moment with Gloria. I thought about that feeling of tension leaving her body as I stepped into her space and touched her hand. A gesture so subtle that no eye could have spotted it, just a hint of pressure, accompanied by a simple question—*Do you really want to do this?*—had opened the possibility that there was a different end to this story than the violent one her gun had set in motion. She answered the question peacefully and in her own truth: *No, I do not.*

I'm not sure if it was in that moment or looking back later, but I began to wonder if there *was* something unique I could offer, or was offering, beyond the food itself, even in my naive state as an outsider. I could arrive and be present without prejudice or assumptions, seeing each and every person as capable of making themselves whole and happy. In short, I could extend to these strangers an attitude of radical trust.

How many others might make different, better choices if they were on the receiving end of a gentle, trusting pressure that flooded them with the belief, or perhaps the memory, that no, they didn't want to do this—*this* being falling victim to the forces that had left them desperately scrambling for food, without shelter, family, resources, or hope? How many times had the new congregants at my church—or, for that matter, struggling people anywhere—experienced the opposite of trust? I thought of all the strangers on the sidewalk, the shopkeepers, the authority figures, the men and women in uniform whose paths they had crossed. I imagined that every time they were watched with suspicious, wary eyes; every time they had been marked with labels that dehumanized them; every time they had been asked to put their hands on a wall or their chest on the pavement; that each of these instances must have walked them incrementally further from the belief that they were worthy of trust or endowed with potential.

I left that day understanding that my journey to help those in crisis would be different and more difficult than in my imaginings. I had a lot to learn. But I also left believing more than ever that the people I'd meet on the street could change their own lives. They just needed someone to extend that gentle pressure.

You can bet I was back out there two nights later, on Thursday evening, as planned. As I laid out the last fixings of my baked-potato bar that night, I noticed there was something missing. On Tuesday, scores of people wandered up and waited as I laid out bowls and utensils. On Thursday, the liquor store parking lot was empty. I looked up and down the street with great curiosity and saw no one moving in our direction. What had I missed? Was there another food line in the neighborhood on Thursday evening? Was there a special event? Bingo, maybe, or a free giveaway at the liquor store?

Half an hour passed, and still not a soul had joined us for dinner.

"Maybe we should pack it up and take the food back to the church," said my helper for the day, shrugging. "We can wrap it up good and put it in the refrigerator for later." Though tempting, leaving didn't feel right.

I walked through the empty lot, up to the sidewalk along Bankhead Highway. Across the street, leaning against a utility pole, I noticed a gentleman. He looked to be in his midfifties, his curly beard graying at the tips, with a handsome, smirking face.

He was looking right at me. His expression wasn't angry or hateful—more like, *What in the world are you doing here?* Making my way through traffic, I crossed the street and extended my hand.

"My name is Bruce; how you doing?"

Slowly he took my hand, shook it firmly, and replied, "Doing just fine, name's Jake." I asked Jake if he'd like some dinner. Dinner sounds good, he said, and we made our way back across the street to the serving line. Jake scooped out double portions of everything, sat his food down, grabbed two cups of lemonade, and proceeded to eat, wasting nothing and grunting his satisfaction now and then.

Jake placed his empty plate on the ground and drained every drop of his second cup of lemonade. He wiped his mouth with his sleeve and exhaled deeply. Looking toward me he nodded slightly, and I knew what the nod meant: "Thank you, that was good, I appreciate it very much." Jake offered no commentary or observations; rather, he simply sat with eyes half-closed, breathing deeper by the moment. I knew I was about to lose him if I didn't speak up.

"Jake, where do you think everyone is today?" I asked, loud enough for him to hear but not so loud as to startle him.

Looking up slowly, smirk returning, Jake asked a question of his own. "You a preacher, ain't you?"

I replied that I was, and Jake laughed deeply and heartily.

"You see," said Jake, "you ain't the first white preacher from up yonder somewhere to come down here planning to help out some folks in trouble. Been plenty like you come through here before. Problem is, every time a little trouble rise up, like Rufus and Gloria the other day, those preachers all pack up and head for home and we don't never see them again." I was surprised to learn Jake had been present for Tuesday's fight; I didn't remember him from the crowd.

"Everybody figured you to be just like the others and nobody thought you'd be coming back here, especially not this soon and probably not ever," he continued.

Looking back at Jake, I made a simple statement that I would have to remind myself and others of many times in the years that followed. "Jake, we come back."

Since we still had a tableful of food, I asked Jake if he would mind walking around and rounding up some folks for the meal. It took him a couple minutes to decide, but he eventually made his way to the corner and started corralling folks. Fifteen minutes later there were forty or more individuals in line, loading up their plates, talking about the weather and sports, saying hello to one another like it was a family reunion. There was no sign of Rufus, but Gloria was present and in good spirits, thanks in large part to the actual spirits she'd consumed throughout the day. No one mentioned Tuesday's dispute. It seemed its only effect was to convince everyone that I'd gotten the heck out of Dodge.

Jake took the lead as the evening moved along. He barked instructions regarding getting second helpings, where the trash should go, who should fold up the tables and chairs. Time and again he introduced me to folks. "This here is the Ghetto Rev, he's a good man, make sure you show some respect."

As the crowd wandered away and we loaded the leftover food, tables, and chairs in the back of the van, Jake looked at me with a real smile.

"See you Tuesday, Ghetto. You'll be back, right?"

NOW I SIT LOOKING BACK, twenty-one years later. Those simple parking lot meals slowly but surely matured into the vision embodied in the name we gave our organization, City of Refuge.

City of Refuge today is a uniquely holistic, full-service program for people in crisis that has now served as the model for successful efforts in ten other cities. We have supported countless thousands of homeless, addicted, and disadvantaged individuals in the 30314 zip code of Atlanta by offering them everything they need, in one place, to move themselves and their children from crisis to dignity and independence.

But as unique and complex as our solution has become, a big part of what makes us different and special is still our emphasis on trusting the people who come through our doors from day one; not in the person who they *will* be, but in the person they *are*. When training our staff, we spend a lot of time hitting home three prerogatives: love everybody, accept everybody, and leave any judgment outside our gates. Every day, in ways both explicit and implicit, we let the people in our programs know they are worthy of our trust and care. We offer them the opportunities they've been lacking and the time they need so that they can learn to trust that their own actions can lead to a better future, amid a community of people who believe in them and lift them up.

Those three words I spoke to Jake in the parking lot—"We come back"—turned out to be remarkably prescient. There's no expiration date on our commitment to people. Trust alone is nothing without time.

You could say that City of Refuge has been the laboratory where together, we (me and thousands of volunteers and recipients of care) have learned trust and relearned it again and again—trust in others; trust in ourselves; trust that we can do things differently tomorrow than we did them today. Together we've seen how trust transforms both parties in the exchange, time and time again. In twenty years of this evolving journey, I've taken away some lessons that I believe aren't just important to helping heal those in need but also to helping heal all of us.

The fact is, trust doesn't come easy to many of us, even those born in loving, secure homes and neighborhoods. We're trust challenged these days in America, and we are increasingly hesitant to share our hearts with others, extending the benefit of the doubt. We're more focused on how we're different than how we're alike. Too much time spent with technology or inside our own homes makes us lonely, and the lonelier we get, the less we trust. Even under the best of circumstances, trusting people we don't know well can be hard to do and even harder to sustain. It requires us to humble ourselves, to make ourselves vulnerable, even at times to risk physical danger, three things that humans are not particularly well adapted to do.

But trust is essential to any human endeavor. Trying to get things done together—whether at your church, your state legislature or municipal government, or your corporate campus—slows to a crawl if people aren't willing to rely on one another. So much time and money is wasted when, facing a trust crisis, we naively attempt to substitute relentless documentation. It's hard to stay focused on actually doing a job well when you're constantly being subjected to new, more onerous methods to prove that you did. Initiative is lost under a pile of paperwork. Leaders who distrust their people inevitably see them fall to the level of their expectations. (And by the way, I've learned, both as a servant to those in crisis and as a boss to now eighty-six employees, that trusting someone doesn't mean you trust they won't screw up—because they will, as will you. You simply trust them to do their best before, during, and after.)

THAT DAY IN THE PARKING LOT, when Gloria put down her gun, I could not have known that she would be a part of our lives for many, many years. Eventually she would lose her health, and then her life, to her alcoholism, one of those too numerous to count who accepted our care but slipped into darkness. Trust and time are powerful forces, but by no means do they transform everyone we work with. Still, we come back.

No one could not have known that Rufus would still be with us today. His transformation happened slowly, but he's now nine years sober. He lives on his own and contributes to his community. He's one of thousands of people I've watched bravely mount the uphill struggle to make their lives better, despite shocking injustices and difficulty. Now he comes back, for others.

When I started City of Refuge, the organization had a tagline: *Light, hope, and transformation for the last, least, and lost.* Some years in, we dropped *for the last, least, and lost.* The closer I got to the people I served, the more I saw it as disrespectful. I wasn't the one providing the transformation, which is what it seemed to imply. I was only improving the conditions for people to transform themselves. I came to realize that it wasn't only the people we served who desire, or need, transformation or an open, trusting heart. It is all of us.

I'm not a politician or a sociologist or someone who pretends to know how to solve the problem of poverty as a nation. I'm only a pastor who decided to commit myself to one zip code in downtown Atlanta. I know only what has worked for us. And though I have made a point to bring many voices into the narrative, I am ultimately telling you my story, from my own point of view. I have learned much over the years, changed much, but I'm still a white, degree-holding pastor from Virginia. I am still at times humbled by my own blind spots. Just like my organization, I'm a work in progress.

In sharing my story, I hope to encourage similar awareness among others and breathe hope into the possibility of healing. As a society we have swung so far from treating our most vulnerable neighbors, and even our peers, with trust, compassion, and benevolent care that it's on us, each of us, to open our arms and our hearts. We all have room to grow.

While radical trust may seem terrifying or even impossible, my experience of founding City of Refuge has convinced me that it is a deeply worthwhile pursuit.

CHAPTER 2

From There to Here

Be sure you put your feet in the right place,
then stand firm.

—ABRAHAM LINCOLN[*]

The neighborhood of Atlanta where City of Refuge is located was one of the city's toughest when I arrived. It still is today. But when I take people on tours of 30314, also home to the parking lot where I served meals, I start in one of its less-pocked corners, near the top of a hill on Sunset Avenue in Vine City. I idle the car outside of an unmarked, nondescript but tidy home that happens to be where Martin Luther King Jr. lived from 1967 until he was assassinated on April 4, 1968.

In his Nobel Lecture in 1964, King famously said, "The time has come for an all-out war against poverty. . . . The poor in our countries have been shut out of our minds, and

---

[*] O. T. Corson, "Abraham Lincoln," *Ohio Educational Monthly* 57 (January 1908): 556.

driven from the mainstream of our societies, because we have allowed them to become invisible."*

Not much has changed in the fifty-five years since he gave that speech. In fact, in 30314 today, things are worse. When King lived in Vine City—now one of the Westside's more infamous hoods, alongside English Avenue, The Bluff, and Hunter Hills, among others—it was a solid, middle-class neighborhood of mostly African American families. Debbie Mois, a resident of English Avenue at that time, recently told me, "Kids could walk back and forth from school and play out in the street after dark. We felt safe. Hot summer nights, the ice-cream truck would come, and it cost six cents to buy a cone. Children could breathe. They didn't feel this constant threat." Most residents were homeowners who took great pride in caring for their homes. And in a time of segregation, black-owned businesses—pharmacies, banks, cinemas, you name it—flourished and met residents' needs. Throughout the '50s and '60s, the neighborhood played a central role in local civil rights efforts.

The gradual victories of integration in the '60s and '70s brought new mobility for those who could afford it. As white Atlantans poured into the suburbs, much of the Westside's middle-class black population upgraded to formerly white neighborhoods. Investors, not families, bought up the prop-

---

* Martin Luther King Jr., "The Quest for Peace and Justice," 1964 Nobel Peace Prize Lecture, https://www.nobelprize.org/prizes/peace/1964/king/lecture.

erties they left behind. Gradually, most of the homes were either rented out, or, as time passed and demand dipped, became "abandominiums"—neglected buildings that enterprising or desperate locals turned into squats, brothels, and trap houses (illegal-drug markets).

In the '80s, crack cocaine hit the neighborhood hard. More recently, heroin became the drug of choice. I was once told that more heroin moves through The Bluff—short for "Better Leave You Effing Fool"—than any other distribution point in the Southeast.

Instead of a War on Poverty, we fought a War on Drugs. Budgets for enforcement and prisons rose like flood waters while money for prevention and treatment went dry. Jail populations ballooned, ultimately leaving Georgia ninth highest in a nation of high imprisonment rates, with five times as many black prisoners as white. I can't tell you how many times we see guys thrown up against cars and think about the kid who won't be seeing her daddy that night, and likely for many nights, months, or years after.

In 1997, when I arrived, buildings were crumbling and there were people living without basic utilities. Crime in the neighborhood got so bad, it was common knowledge that there were streets that ambulances would refuse to service.

Why am I telling you all this? In part, to help you understand the larger context of misery in this corner of the world. King was right: Allowing these people and their lives to be invisible traps them in the margins. But also because I see how the War on Drugs has contributed to the total breakdown of trust in communities like mine. When you recast black teenage boys as "superpredators" and replace treatment for addicts with extreme mandatory sentences, you criminalize the vulnerable and divide people in fear. Where trust expands possibilities, an overemphasis on enforcement shrinks them to the paces of a jail cell, not just for the prisoners but for the families and friends who mourn their absence.

So that's the status on trust in 30314. But let's talk about where you live. In any zip code, anywhere, *trust* is more challenging to muster than many other qualities, such as compassion, empathy, and patience, we all hope to extend to people we interact with. That's because trust is *dynamic*. It's two-way, and therefore immediately forces us to cede or share control. If compassion is like driving a car with passengers at your side, trust is like hood-riding, an adventure that ends quickly and potentially painfully if your partners aren't up to the ride.

When people hear my story, they're often more curious to hear how I earned trust than how I extended it. The short answer is *time*. I put in a lot of it. But in the early days, for a white pastor from the suburbs, winning trust required a lot of improvising. As elsewhere, being a religious figure could work for me or against me depending on the individual, and there was no way to tell which group someone fell into. When a new person came into my office—let's say a sixteen-year-old black teenage boy, there because a judge decided to send him to me instead of to jail for dealing drugs—I would welcome him warmly, then relax back in my chair. As much as I could, I let him do the talking. I listened. I kept my own demeanor calm, my gaze open. I kept my words and my thinking grounded in those three things I believe are foundational to trust: love, acceptance, and a nonjudgmental attitude. Would he start to trust me in that hour? Probably not. But I was creating the space for him to come to me next time a little less angry, a little more curious about who I was and what I might have to offer.

Truthfully, though, I think my hood-riding past explains better than anything else how I "got" trust so readily. If you don't know what hood-riding is, maybe you didn't spend a winter in Brown Town, Virginia, on the Jackson family farm as a child. We'd rub down an old car hood with soap, drag it up a big hill like hillbilly bobsledders, then take our positions around the perimeter, holding onto the edges, and sometimes onto one another, for dear life as we hurtled down the slope, narrowly missing trees and rocks and hoping to stop before being baptized in the creek's icy waters.

Success in hood-riding requires a delicate balance. The majority of the weight needs to be on the front half with just enough weight on the back to keep the hood from tipping forward. Too much weight on the front and the slightest bump will cause the rear end to fly up, catapulting the riders into the air. Too much weight on the back and the air will cause the front of the hood to lift, flipping over backward and potentially landing on the riders. Though fun to watch from a distance, neither of these scenarios is exciting to be part of. Just ask Tracy White, who lost part of a finger when the edge of the hood came down on his hand.

Learning to trust your fellow hood riders is essential to arriving at the bottom of the hill safely. One misplaced fourth grader and all hell breaks loose. One person who allows fear to rule the moment and to override the confidence of "holding your position" can cause pain, not only to themselves but to everyone riding the hood. You have to trust people to hold their positions all the way down—and they have to trust you.

That's what trust can feel like—possible loss of digits, if not of life itself—when it's new and fresh and anything real is on the line. You're immediately cured of the foolish belief that you hold all the power. Lose the trust of one person, whether in you or in the process, and suddenly you're head-down in snow.

Looking back, there were many aspects of my childhood that helped to prepare me for the life work I chose. My dad was a preacher who was most satisfied when he was traveling from church to church, sharing the good news and helping people along their road to spiritual recovery. He would schedule meeting after meeting, sometimes weeks on end, and travel with his small family—Mom, me, and my brother, Jeff, who is thirteen months younger than I am. We would stay in church parsonages or cheap motels, eat what was offered or what we could afford, and collect small "offerings" from the few folks who showed up to hear the traveling evangelist purport the good news. Jeff and I would often fall asleep on hard wooden pews as church services went long into the night. Dad would carry us to the car, and after a night of rest, we would find ways to pass the time until the next service began. This may seem monotonous or even painful for a boy of five or six, but in my mind I was living a high adventure—seeing new sights, meeting new folks, sleeping in strange places. We relied constantly on the goodwill of strangers to survive, and I got plenty of experience being an outsider. "Home" was a daily parade of new faces and spaces, with our family offering the gravity to keep our feet planted.

As a child I was slight of build, had bright red hair and freckles, and seemed to attract unsavory characters looking for opportunities to bully kids they perceived to be weak. Rather than run and hide or try to talk the bullies out of harassing me, my approach was to hit first, hit hard, and hit last. Maybe the lack of fear was instilled in me by my father, Cecil, a rough-and-tumble man raised "up the holler" in West Virginia. His father, my grandpa Henry, was as crusty as the bark on the trees he harvested from the mountains.

He'd cut them down by hand, hook them by chain to a mule, and drag them down uneven, rocky land to the sawmill. Hard work, hard drinking, and hard living defined Grandpa for most of his life. While my dad chose a different path, the genes of Henry Deel lived not too deep beneath the surface. Now and again they would remind us they were there. My bloodline was part Henry and part Cecil; therefore, running *into* instead of *away from* was the way I chose to handle bullies, fights, and other challenges. Little did I know that those encounters, most won and a few lost, were preparing me for my life's work.

When I was six years old, my brother Keith was born. Dad decided it would be wise to settle down and lead one church rather than travel with a growing family or leave us home as he continued an itinerate ministry. While this brought some level of normalcy to our lives, Dad was rarely content for very long and we moved often. I attended ten schools in twelve years and each move brought a new set of bullies that required me to prove myself again. Whether it was the day a thug from a rival school placed the barrel of a 16-gauge shotgun against my lower lip and dared me to speak, or the day my friend Jason and I tried to maim each other with two-by-four planks in shop class, or the day during my junior year when I found myself in a full-blown fistfight with my school bus driver, I am grateful to have survived.

I was never considered the smartest kid in the class or

the best athlete on the field. No one ever marveled at my potential. Those who knew me from a distance concluded that I was an introvert—an arrogant one, maybe, with a bit of a sharp edge. Those who chose to see the best in me saw a nonconformist risk-taker, one who was willing to defend the weak and stand up to bullies. None of that really mattered because of two things. One, I had been so many places and seen so many people that I wasn't too tied to what any one person thought. And two, I always had my dad behind me, cheering me on, letting me know that his expectations for me were high and he trusted I would meet them.

That said, I don't claim to have had any big dreams, lofty goals, or idealistic agendas myself. Growing up, I simply worked daily to embrace the moment, to push the edge of what was deemed acceptable, to laugh, to reflect, and if necessary, to fight for the right to do so.

My journey after high school took me to Lee University, a Christian college in Cleveland, Tennessee, where I eventually decided I would follow in my father's footsteps and become a minister. It was far from a foregone conclusion. Even a Christian college provided opportunities and liberties to which I had never been exposed. Suffice it to say my mind was not always sharp and clear when I sat down at eight a.m. for a study in Systematic Theology.

Academically speaking, I barely survived college. But I did develop friendships that would last a lifetime, and I honed a work ethic that was a means to survival. I never called home for money. Dad and Mom lived on a meager income, and a baby girl, April, had taken my seat at the table. So I worked. I delivered newspapers, officiated basketball and softball games, painted houses, and worked the third shift at the Holiday Inn as a night auditor. I unloaded tractor-trailer loads of candy at a local distribution warehouse and drove a forklift in a factory. If you lived in my dad's house, you were going to work—and anyway, I never felt comfortable sitting around doing nothing. My near-total lack of acquaintance with something I've heard about called "leisure" turned out to be the right background for starting and growing a crisis-focused nonprofit.

Rhonda Ramsey transferred to Lee the summer after my sophomore year. Of the many things that attracted me to her, the fact that she was not afraid of work was near the top of the list. Like myself, she depended on no one to help her make it through college. Rhonda worked on campus during the day and off campus in the evenings. She was a diligent student and was involved in campus activities, often in leadership roles. We connected in many ways, and one of those ways was that we both understood the importance of hard work. Depending on others was a foreign concept. Although our dating journey would take many twists and turns, I know without a doubt that the attitude we both possessed regarding life and what was required to succeed kept drawing us together.

After college I entered the field of traditional ministry and became a youth pastor in a small church in Baton Rouge, Louisiana. The pastor wore loud suits with big pockets sewn on the sides of the jackets and ties that had designs of birds, clouds, and other elements of God's creation. He was cousin to Jerry Lee Lewis, Mickey Gilley, and Jimmy Swaggart, and he played piano like we were in the juke joint down the road. I was a fish out of water and hated Louisiana's heat and bugs. I lasted a grand total of eight months on my first assignment and headed back east in a hurry. Over the next few years I served churches in Tampa, Florida; Snellville and Augusta, Georgia; and Pulaski, Virginia; before accepting a position just north of Atlanta where I served as youth and associate pastor. It was during my tenure there that I started leading groups into tough neighborhoods in downtown Atlanta. We fed homeless folks, passed out clothing and blankets and hygiene kits, and held carnivals for kids in at-risk environments. We painted and repaired homes and gave away school supplies.

It was good work done with the right motive, but there was a sense that we were putting bandages on heart attacks. I'd head into the city and spend a few hours on a Saturday handing out toiletries and sandwiches to people who diverted their eyes from mine, knowing I was someone they'd never met and who they'd probably never meet again. That's how I experienced it anyway, alongside the sinking feeling that the "good" we were doing had an even shorter shelf life than the bologna in the sandwiches. Afterward I'd go home and quickly forget what I'd seen and felt, until the next time. These superficial efforts weren't healing or transforming anyone, either those we served or ourselves. Friends and others in ministry told me that helping people in crisis was the right thing to do, so we did it, but I felt unsettled in the work and in the life I was living.

By that time, I was long and happily married to Rhonda. We had four daughters. Our home was Stone Mountain, thirty minutes north from downtown Atlanta, in a relatively affluent neighborhood where kids played safely in the streets. Rhonda pulled our girls to school every morning in a Radio Flyer wagon, and she remembers our home there as the prettiest she'd ever known.

The neighborhood was quaint, but I found it somewhat sterile. I knew in my heart that my life and work were not making a positive difference to the people who were just a hop away, people who faced tremendous challenges, obstacles, and adversity in life. Little did I know major change was on the horizon.

OUT OF THE BLUE, I was asked to take a six-month break from my staff position at the church in North Atlanta and speak on Sunday mornings at a small church in the city. The Mission, as it was once called, was on the verge of closing down. It had a handful of loyal parishioners and very little money. I was given the assignment to evaluate the current

situation and determine if the church should be shut down
and the property closed.

My new assignment was on Fourteenth Street, northwest
of the roughest of Atlanta's neighborhoods, and just north of
Georgia Tech. Two blocks away stood the other bulwark of
the neighborhood, the Al-Farooq Masjid mosque, which had
a healthy and growing congregation of residents from all
over Atlanta.

The neighborhood was far from the worst hood in Atlanta but was wearing signs of neglect. As elsewhere, most
folks with two nickels to rub together, white or black, had
abandoned the inner city for the suburbs. The neighborhood
was depressed and transient; people passed through, looking
for a place to use drugs or for something to thieve.

The church had been founded in 1969 as an outreach
mission, with parishioners living dormitory-style with the
homeless. Eventually it evolved into a more traditional church,
serving a white middle-class congregation. By 1997, those parishioners had all married, had kids, and moved to the suburbs. The handful that still came to the Mission were commuting
in every Sunday. They were committed to one another, but the
neighborhood where they worshipped had become more of
an inconvenience than a calling.

The third floor of the sixty-five-year-old building offered
a great view of the surrounding community, which was characterized by small, ugly houses lined up like LEGOs, each one

nearly touching the next. Beyond, we could see downtown, with its formidable, gleaming skyscrapers and the massive Georgia Dome arena. The view offered a snapshot of our city but also of the world at large—poverty next door to wealth, hopelessness rubbing shoulders with tremendous success, desperation parallel to affluence.

My intention was to serve well for six months and return to our nice, stable suburban life. On the fifth or sixth Sunday of my assignment, a lady who looked like she had not slept in several nights walked in the back door during services. She stood out in the crowd of a couple dozen folks and instantly became the object of conspicuous glances. She ignored them and held her ground. After the service ended, she walked down the aisle, took me by the hand, and began to weep. Through tears, she looked in my eyes and said, "I've been hooking and stripping fourteen years. Can you help me get out?"

I shared a prayer with her, and in the days that followed, I helped her find a safe place to stay, purchased her some clothes, and gave her money for a bus pass and food. She came to services again that next Sunday and brought one of her former clients with her, a man who was in an alcoholic crisis of his own. That started a pattern that would last for several months. We would show up on Sunday to be greeted by homeless folks, drug addicts, and neighbors with a host of other life-challenging issues. What began with one request

from one little lady became a chorus of precious human beings crying out, "Can you help us?"

Approximately four months in to what I thought was a
six-month assignment, I walked in on a Sunday morning and
nearly a hundred people whose lives were characterized by
deep struggle were gathered. They had invited one another,
promising one person after another that the preacher at the
church down the street would help. When we passed the
offering plate, it often received more than crumbled bills. Baggies of crack, syringes, and even once a semiautomatic weapon
were among the contraband that our new brothers and sisters offered up, seeking to make a change.

The first few times someone made such an offering, I may
have gone a little bug-eyed. It wasn't apprehension so much
as surprise. Any negative emotion quickly switched to awe
when I considered how much these sacrifices meant to their
owners. With our congregation as witness, they were making
a commitment to a new path and were often overwhelmed
with emotion. Very quickly, when someone put drugs or
whatever else in the offering plate, the congregation's reac-
tion shifted from the uneasy surprise of the first time to immediate and raucous cheering. It became a ritual celebration
of a new friend's decision to make a positive life change.

If anything made me apprehensive, it wasn't drug paraphernalia. It was the weight of responsibility I now felt to
these folks who had given up their crutch and taken our

hands. Could I really help them, beyond the initial flush of hope? I honestly didn't know yet. All I knew for sure was one, they were asking me to, and two, that I could and would receive them with acceptance and work as hard as I ever had to find resources. I had the strong feeling that something important had begun, and I knew I couldn't turn my back on it.

After many conversations with Rhonda, I wrangled my uncertainty and made the call to resign from the church I had served for more than five years. I accepted the pastorate of the little church in downtown Atlanta. Not long after, I filed paperwork to launch a nonprofit designed to assist those experiencing various forms of crisis. It was obvious to me that, while God might have a role to play, this community needed more than spiritual guidance. The church where I was serving may have been called the Mission, but I had not gone there as a missionary. Helping others was its own end, and a relationship with a benevolent God a potential piece in the puzzle of healing.

To quote MLK once more, "True neighborliness requires personal concern."* In his sermon on the Good Samaritan, MLK points out that what he gave the stranger on the road was more than just his hands to bind the wounds but also an "overflowing of love to bind up the wounds of his broken spirit." But here I was in new territory with no personal ref-

---

* Martin Luther King Jr., *Strength to Love* (Minneapolis: Fortress Press, 2010), 28.

erence point from which to draw. I had to start somewhere. It seemed like serving meals was the best way to meet an immediate need while getting to know people, so that someday we might share more than a transaction of calories. I would begin a pattern of meals on the same days and times each week, Tuesday and Thursday evenings, so that our hungry friends would know a hot meal would always be waiting.

In the world of poverty-focused nonprofits, this was a "street feeding." Street feedings are meant to solve a simple problem: hunger. Sometimes, out of convenience, we adopted that lingo, but I never liked it. We hoped that people would leave our meals feeling not just less hungry but more human. I wanted these meals to start to close the distance between us. I still knew little about what people on the street really needed, but maybe this could create the conditions for me to learn.

It occurred to me pretty quickly that offering peanut butter or bologna sandwiches on stale bread that had been donated from the local grocery in an attempt to befriend the community was contradictory to our vision. I decided on food of good quality, served fresh and hot. If we served breakfast, for example, it would be sausage or bacon, real eggs cracked, whipped, and cooked by hand, pancakes with syrup, juice and hot coffee with cream and sugar—just like breakfast at my house or that of the volunteers serving alongside me. Every person going through the line would be treated with respect. We would learn their names and find out if they liked their coffee black, light, or light and sweet. This was how we'd put dignity on the menu.

Meanwhile, we began an after-school program to feed twenty kids from low-income, high-risk environments while we tutored them in their studies. At the end of each session, we loaded them up in a van and took them home to some of the worst housing complexes imaginable. After-school programming led to summer programming and then to Christmas events and field trips and weeklong camp experiences.

Twenty kids quickly became forty, then sixty, and the numbers continued to grow. Putting more than a hundred kids and parents on a forty-four-passenger bus to transport them from their housing complex to our ministry center was illegal and dangerous, but doing so seemed not so much riskier than the front yards they left behind. We had a great time singing, laughing, and learning dozens of nicknames. Everybody in 30314, it seemed, had one—none of which we created, and a few of which gave us pause. But if Fat Mama and Miss Johnson (Molly and LaRhonda, ages four and five), Phat Man (Oliver, ten), and his brothers Milkman (Shontavious, seven) and Mon (Marquez, five), to give just a few examples, were offended by the names their families had assigned them, they sure didn't show it. I came to understand the nicknames as terms of endearment within a private, familiar language of family and friends.

It cracks your heart open to see kids in need. While

checking heads for lice at one of our first summer camps, the camp nurse discovered crusty scabs covering the scalp of one of the little girls. Upon further inspection, she realized that the child's hair had not been washed in months and her scalp was covered with dirt, sores, and scabs. We also realized that the girl had come to camp without a single change of clothes and no bedding or shower items. Rhonda and I went to town and purchased five outfits, including shorts, shirts, undergarments, a bathing suit, and sandals. We also bought medicated shampoo. We returned to camp and gave the items to the girl's counselor. The counselor put on her bathing suit and had the little girl do the same. Together they got in the shower and the counselor washed and rinsed with the medicated shampoo. Over and over she gently massaged the shampoo into the child's hair and rinsed away the debris. After an hour, she began to tenderly brush the child's hair, slowly moving through a section at a time until the job was finished.

A few hours later I was in the chapel preparing for the evening gathering when a beautiful little girl whom I did not recognize walked in the back door. She was dressed in a pretty purple outfit and white sandals. I recognized it as one of the outfits Rhonda had chosen. Her hair was clean and styled with half a dozen white bows. She walked down the aisle and with a big grin on her face, looked up at me and asked, "Pastor Bruce, am I pretty?" I fought back tears and knelt in front of her. I took her by the hands and said,

"Darling, you are beautiful." A smile burst onto her face but was short lived, quickly replaced by worry. She asked, "Do I get to keep these clothes, or do I have to give them back when I go home?"

Her question floored me. It had never occurred to any of us to let her know that the clothes were a gift. I assured her they were hers to keep. The smile burst back and she gave me a hug to rival all hugs. She turned and skipped proudly out of the building.

This camp felt like a million miles from the church camp I attended for many summers in Roanoke as a child. Most of the kids were from working-class families, but there were a handful of boys who came with a new pair of jeans and a new shirt for each day of the week, often with their names carefully monogrammed onto their clothing by their mothers. I'm sure some of them would take advantage of being away from parental governance for a few days to stop bathing and washing their hair, but you can be sure their mothers took them in hand when they arrived home. I myself never thought about not having clothes or shoes or a toothbrush. We didn't have much, but cleanliness was next to godliness, and there were serious mandates regarding both. Mom packed everything I needed. I never gave a thought to the possibility that somewhere else, some other child might have shown up with nothing but scabs and need.

My exchange with that little girl, whose experience in her

few years of life was so different already from my own, hit
me hard.

As time passed, I started to understand that these kids
had never experienced the steady, secure ground that predis-
poses a person to trust, in individuals, institutions, or themselves. Today the U.S. has one of the highest child poverty
rates in the developed world. In our corner of Atlanta,
40 percent of families live below the federal poverty line.
Many kids I was singing with on the bus were born into an
environment of anxiety and opportunity injustice. Mom
didn't graduate high school, Dad may or may not have been
in the picture. They were seeing drug use all around them,
SWAT teams, and family members dragged away in handcuffs.
There was food insecurity. Inadequate educational opportunity. Violent crime. Institutions that were quick to punish
but slow to aid. These kids were growing up without the opportunity to build identity, self-esteem, and dignity. Our
parents' love is the foundation for this, but what happens
when Mom can barely take care of herself?

Kids without positive role models and encouragement
forge their identity out of negative labels stamped on them by
others. You're the child of a single-parent household; that's
your first label. Your father's a criminal; that's a label. You're
a dropout; that's a label. You're homeless; that's a label. You're
an addict; that's a label. All these labels add up, and without
any other message to counteract them, folks internalize and

act on the belief that they aren't worthy. They stop trusting their ability to shape their own future.

Meeting these kids felt like traveling back in time. It flooded me with empathy for the adults we were meeting, many of whom had grown up in similar environments, or worse. Meanwhile, when Bruce Deel entered this world, it was like God had thrown down a welcome mat, though I might not always have seen it that way. I was surrounded with love and opportunities that made trust easy. If I worked hard and made good choices, I could be reasonably sure of good outcomes. Where I was now, people were born into struggle. Trusting that things could be different, or that someone wanted to help, came hard—which made it all the more heart-rending every time I saw someone take a chance on me and a chance on themselves.

IN THOSE EARLIEST DAYS of City of Refuge, dishing food out in the parking lot, I found myself thinking often to the Old Testament scroll of 2 Samuel, which is better known as the story of David and Goliath. Jesse had eight sons, and all but David, the youngest, were with the Israelite army, preparing to go to war against their most formidable enemy, the Philistines. A giant named Goliath had interfered with their battle plans, so there they were on the front lines with no battles fought, no war won, no victory to brag about.

Jesse put together a package of items for David to deliver to his brothers. Inside were bread, wine, and ten varieties of cheese. There was nothing for fighting—no weapons, no battle plans, no shields or swords; only what to modern ears sounds like a fairly gourmet picnic spread. David's mission wasn't strategic support for killing Goliath or defeating the Philistines. It was to be an expression of family, caring for sons and brothers with a meal that provided not just sustenance but pleasure. Food and drink and conversation, that's the sum total of the plan Jesse had when he sent David along with the package, setting the stage for one of history's greatest underdog stories.

We all know how the story ends. David asks the king for permission to fight the giant. He's roundly mocked and ridiculed, but since no soldier steps up, the king relents. It turns out that while David may be small, he's mighty with a slingshot. He makes his way to the giant, who now takes *his* turn in taunting him. With incredible accuracy, David releases the first stone from the sling and hits Goliath in the forehead, dropping the towering soldier to the ground. Then David puts a giant exclamation point on the victory by using Goliath's own sword to cut off his head. In an instant David brought victory to the Israelite army, and his legend lives thousands of years later, all because he had the audacity to decide he could do more than carry a picnic basket.

When I first thought about the story, I will admit I

identified with the hero. Like David, I was going about my life, fulfilling my duty, when I was asked to take bread and cheese to some folks who were in trouble. I'd never done battle on the field of addiction, never rescued a victim of sex trafficking, never stared down a thief holding something he had stolen from my children. But I didn't run. Experience had already taught me that I was worthy of the battle.

It took some time to realize that people fighting giants of homelessness, addiction, incarceration, and poverty needed a David as much as they needed a garage door opener. Sure, they needed bread and cheese. But then, belly full, they needed someone to help them see that they themselves could be David. They, too, could best their giant. Take that little girl at our summer camp. Her confidence blossomed after that day she approached me with bows in her hair. When the children sang together, she pushed her way to the front every time. Some of that was the effect of the new clothes, but what lifted her even more, I think, was the overflowing of love she experienced in those hours she spent held and groomed by gentle hands.

What each person needed, practically speaking, would look different—but they all needed an overflowing of love that would give them faith that they could face their giants, ignoring whatever voices throughout their lives had told them otherwise.

If transformation were ever to come, they would be the hero of their own story. I could believe in them all I wanted—but they would need to believe it, too.

CHAPTER 3

Commune and Communion

Pope Francis . . . says that communion is not some
grand prize for the perfect person but rather
food for the hungry one.

—FATHER GREG BOYLE[*]

P eople think of lack of empathy as an emotional deficit, but in truth, it's just as often a knowledge deficit. How can you walk in a man's shoes when you're not even sure what they look like? Early in the journey of City of Refuge, I found out that the more I closed the distance between myself and those I hoped to help, the easier trust came. You can't give someone the side-eye when they're right smack in front of you. And the more I closed the distance, the more my empathy grew. I began to understand poverty as a cause, not an effect, of bad decisions.

One surefire way to close emotional distance: Put your

---

[*] Gregory Boyle, *Barking to the Choir* (New York: Simon & Schuster, 2018), 123.

own skin in the game. Demonstrating commitment with action makes brothers of strangers; colleagues of employees; even friends of foes. I have my wife, Rhonda, to thank for this understanding. She's the one who decided, just months after we started the parking lot meals, that it was time to literally close the distance between us and our new friends. We were about to transition from two addresses to one, and what a transition it would be.

At the time we were living in our affluent suburban enclave, in a beautiful three-story home with a fantastic front porch and a spacious deck in the back. Decades-old hardwoods covered the property, and a tire swing hung from one of the giant limbs. The swing was one of the favorite things about our place for our three oldest girls, Kassi, Kelsi, and Kensi, then ages seven, five, and three. Our fourth daughter, Kaylin, was just a year old, and Rhonda would sit on the deck and hold her while I pushed one of the older siblings in the swing. The other girls ran and played as if they didn't have a care in the world. I was driving to and from the city each day to serve bread and cheese. Rhonda, who had left the corporate world to become a full-time mother, would join me with the girls on Sundays when we headed down to the little church for the weekly service.

The morning our lives changed still shines brightly in my memory. I was in my office in the city and the desk phone rang (this was when we still used desk phones). Rhonda was on the line and I quickly detected emotion in her voice. Concerned, I waited for what I assumed might be bad news. As it turned out, she had just finished her morning reflection time and had sensed that a change should take place, a huge change.

Gently, yet firmly, she spoke. "If we are really going to impact a city, we have to be *in* the city," she said. *I am in the city*, I thought. She pressed on. "I think we need to move downtown. We need to be among the people," she said. "We have to live there so we can know them better and they can trust us. It's not enough just to drive in now and then, we have to be there."

Just when I thought I had figured some stuff out—bread and cheese and empowering others—Rhonda had leaped straight to the real deal. She had been feeling the tug every time we drove back home to our comforts, leaving far behind the people we claimed to want to transform with compassion. I thought about what Jake had said about pastors coming and going. Why should anybody take my expressions of commitment seriously when really I had committed so little? We were still interlopers, not neighbors. We were looking *at* the people we served, and they at us, instead of everybody looking forward together. And when we looked at them, it was not without blame, if I'm really honest. On some level I still believed they were the primary architects of their own crises.

Rhonda was right. If we wanted to make good on our vision for City of Refuge, we had to move. I was not expecting a radical lifestyle change during my thirty-seventh year of life, but here I was. I had started our nonprofit believing we could bring light, hope, and transformation to people living on the margins. I hadn't banked on the fact that the first big transformation would be mine. With Rhonda's urging, we would upend everything we thought about the life we were going to live. This was both exhilarating and sobering.

The nonprofit was not yet generating enough donations to cover the cost of the work we were doing and provide a salary for me at the same time. The little church I was pastoring was generating some income, and after paying the note on the building, utilities, insurance, and other miscellaneous bills, there was a small amount left that I drew as compensation. When I looked at the closest "nice" neighborhoods near the mission, I quickly discovered that the cost of living was out of reach. When I found homes that were within budget, they were in not-so-nice neighborhoods that I couldn't convince myself to move my daughters into. Houses we could afford needed major repair, or were located in extremely high crime zones, or both.

Rhonda, again, provided the answer. We were walking through the empty third floor of the church, one day, when we both stopped and looked at the cavernous space with new eyes.

"It's completely empty," I said.

"Let's move in," she answered. And just like that, it was decided.

Among the foundational problems with this idea was that churches aren't constructed to accommodate family living. The floor was set up as twin dormitories. Each had a tiny kitchen, bathrooms with showers, and a large, open central space that would become the living room, dining room, and play area. As is common to older church buildings, the windows were made of stained glass—but if you're imagining the light shining through beautiful artistic scenes of angels, stop there. These were just dim, rectangular panes of purple-brown glass, aside from the ones that had been broken, replaced, and painted over an even duller brown. Even in midday, the dormitory was bathed in dark gloom. The group bathrooms, with their rows of urinals and showers, were so dark and dank Rhonda started calling them the Wicked Bathrooms.

We were only there a few days before Rhonda exclaimed, "I have to be able to see outside!" Thankfully, I found a putty knife and was able to scrape the paint off a few panes of glass, letting in outside light. One night, we were fast asleep in bed when we woke to the sound of glass shattering, then felt and heard something hard hit the headboard of our bed. Rhonda and I both rolled instinctively onto the floor, terrified and confused and half-asleep. Almost immediately, another pane of glass shattered, and I saw a chunk of asphalt hit the floor. Fear shifted to bewilderment as I crawled to another of the windows and peered out. A man, so drunk he could barely stand, was hurling chunks of broken pavement. At that point, bewilderment became anger. So what if *we* were afraid; what if it had been the girls' room? My feet carried me outside. I screamed him off the property with a baseball bat.

By the next morning, we had already begun to put the tension behind us; it almost seemed like it had been a dream. Except now, direct sunlight streamed through the broken panes in our bedroom. As we sat there admiring it, we decided he maybe had done us a favor.

Looking outside was better than the alternative, but the view was not the thing that nature photographers are scouring the land for. Outside the master bedroom, just feet from the building, was a four-lane, heavily traveled street. Twenty-four hours a day vehicles passed by. The sound of sirens rang out often but we quickly adapted, tuning out the police or fire vehicles as they zoomed through the neighborhood. The conversations taking place as folks walked along the sidewalk were easily heard and we always knew when conflict was happening. The views from the girls' bedroom and the family room were no better, as this glorious vista consisted of the church parking lot and dumpy houses that lined the street. In the spirit of choose your battles, we didn't gripe at the neighbors who viewed our parking lot as their own, even the neighbor who graced us with his 1970s hearse that had been converted into a party wagon and painted in bright, Funkadelic style.

———

BEFORE WE COULD START the process of bringing light, hope, and transformation, I had to figure out how to make life work in an old church building with four little girls and no bathtub. There was also the minor issue of having a couple of homeless guys camped out on the front porch smoking crack, and having the aroma and smoke ease its way underneath the door where a seal once existed. To address the bath issue I purchased a #2 washtub and a water hose. The two youngest girls had a blast playing in the metal washtub and being rinsed off with a green water hose. I had a "chat" with the guys on the front porch and requested they relocate. To them relocation meant flipping their blankets to face the opposite direction, so I figured I'd better let it go for the moment, given I was the new guy in the neighborhood.

We never knew if it was those guys or someone else, but the first night we stayed in the building someone tried to steal our van by hot-wiring it. As it turns out they must've been too incapacitated by their drug of choice and actually hot-wired the windshield wipers. When I walked out the following morning, the van was still there and the wipers were going—left to right, right to left. Little did I know that this criminal activity would be the first of many incidents we would experience over the next six years of life in the church.

We settled in a bit and started to make the space feel like

home. A couple weeks after moving in I left my office one day and went upstairs for a quick lunch break. As I entered the living area I called out to Rhonda to let her know I was in the house. She didn't respond, so I began to walk the space and call her name. We had stored some items on the unfinished fourth floor of the building so I made my way there to see if Rhonda might need help carrying down boxes to be unpacked. As I came into the space I heard the sound of crying in the far corner behind a small mountain of boxes. I quietly eased over, and as I looked around the boxes, I saw my beautiful wife sitting in a chair, head bowed, weeping.

In our ten years together, I had rarely seen her cry. Startled, I stood there for what seemed like several minutes and finally stepped to her side. I knelt down and gently embraced her. I wasn't sure why she was crying but I knew it wasn't the time for me to ask questions or offer advice. I felt I should just be with her. After a few minutes, she pulled herself together and pointed to two boxes she needed taken down. Without missing a beat, she got back to the business of unpacking and setting up our home.

Later we revisited the experience. In the dust and darkness of the attic, surrounded by cardboard boxes holding the relics of our beautiful former home, with the great yard and cool tire swing, she was overcome with emotion. No matter how sure she was of this new life, she needed to grieve the loss of her old one. After ten years of happy domesticity, we had now moved into a place of dust motes, cracked linoleum, and exposed plywood floors, where the bugs were rat-sized, and the rats were cat-sized. But all that was inconsequential compared to the real change at hand. We had decided to give our lives over to a population of people who are often ignored by just about everyone else, including many of the people who had populated our old life.

After giving herself time to weep, Rhonda felt her spirit shift. *All right, ready for the next thousand miles,* she thought—and off she went, leaving me in awe.

We enrolled the girls in school. Through an incredible, providential turn of events, they had been accepted into a nearby private elementary school with the majority of tuition covered by scholarships. Each morning the older girls would dress in plaid jumpers and either Rhonda or I would drop them off in a safe, spotless, successful environment where they would interact with kids from families who lived in beautiful homes and had parents with great careers. Every evening we would pick them up from school and return to an ancient church building with burglar bars on the windows and asphalt for a yard. Sometimes the girls would have friends over after school. The looks on the faces of their parents were priceless when they showed up to get their kids. Sometimes friends would come once and never come back. I suppose the parents were not the adventurous type.

Life in the church *was* an adventure. Rhonda was fond of

saying we should sell wristbands. The sanctuary became the girls' playground, and rappelling from the balcony and swimming in the baptistery seemed acceptable, not blasphemous as some would charge. At night and in the early morning, the girls would watch the parking lot from their third-floor dormer windows like they had front-row seats at a movie—and not a G-rated one either. They saw all kinds of action, from backseat romance to criminal mischief. I never knew when I might hear a chirpy, little girl voice shout, "Daddy, somebody's down there with a crowbar!" Our fifth daughter, Karli, was born while we lived in the church. Her nursery, as you can probably guess, looked nothing like the quiet, orderly nooks you see photographed in parenting magazines.

As soon as we were settled in, we started inviting folks to the Streetlight Café, an area in the church that had at one time been used as a Christian gathering place for Georgia Tech students. Now the space created the opportunity to have Jake or Rufus or one of a hundred other friends over for dinner and fellowship—much better ambiance than a parking lot, with a piano to boot. Our volunteers made simple meals in the kitchen, but we took things up a notch by creating a dessert station, with cheesecakes and other goodies we got from a nearby bakery. The desserts, combined with a donated cappuccino machine, made it feel more like a special event, or even a restaurant. It felt good to host our newfound friends in a more intimate setting, and the number grew rapidly.

The people around the table were a jumble of backgrounds. Homeless folks sat next to upper-middle-class suburbanites, who sat next to Georgia Tech students, who sat next to falling-down-drunk alcoholics. We decided to focus conversation on those things that everybody could comfortably talk about: Atlanta sports, the weather, the food, and such. These topics may sound mundane or superficial, but to our friends in crisis, they were a profound gift. At last, here were "respectable" people who hadn't immediately started lecturing them on what needed to be fixed in their lives. Meal by meal, the people we ate with began to see that we were genuinely interested in getting to know them, as they were. Slowly, they began to trust in the potential of friendship. Time and time again we saw this incredible transformation take place, and years of distrust, anger, and frustration fell away over hot food and warm conversation.

We volunteers felt our own understanding shift in the course of these dinners. Any residual feeling of "us and them" disappeared. The mood shifted from "How do we help *them*?" to "How do we do this together?" And from there, my extension of trust went from being theoretical to practical. I might, for example, hand the keys to our valuable storage room to a homeless recent crack addict. An outsider might watch this and think, *Is he crazy?* No, I wasn't—because I wasn't giving keys to a crack addict. I was giving them to a man who I knew liked cherry pie better than cheesecake, who had bumped my elbow dozens of times while we ate a hearty meal, and whom I had watched pat my youngest daughter's cheek so gently my eyes welled with tears. In short, I was giving them to a friend, one endowed with all the dignity of that relationship.

As our community of guests grew, so did our pool of volunteers—both at our meals and at our after-school and summer programs for kids. Jake and Gloria had become self-appointed security guards who helped to maintain crowd control and keep order. Neither of them was afraid to speak strongly to those who would disrupt. Most of our other volunteers were drawn from the church's congregation. Most, but not all, were newcomers. I had gotten plenty of phone calls and knocks on my office door from the church's original parishioners, who told me they didn't feel comfortable anymore in the pews they had sat in for decades. "We didn't sign up for this" was pretty much the attitude toward my welcoming of people in crisis, and I didn't begrudge or judge them. What would be the point? I wasn't unsympathetic to their feelings, but I was committed to serving the community with a radically inclusive approach. As time passed, all but a few stalwart souls would leave.

Even more came. Longtime members like Jim and Mary

joined resources with new folks. My brother Jeff and his family returned from doing mission work in Jamaica and joined the effort. Many others, too many to count and some names forgotten along the way, came bringing bread and cheese.

Moving into the church turned out to be a bright neon sign of commitment not just to the people we were helping but also to potential volunteers, who were now showing up in a steady flow. Not all of them stayed, of course, but as they say, every effort is an effort, and City of Refuge exists thanks to all the people who pitched in along the way. We welcomed even what you might call the tourists, in great numbers. This type of volunteer, plentiful but short-lived, heard about the crazy preacher and his family who had moved into a church and were hanging out in unsavory places in the city. They wanted to see this, to get a view on what it looked like to truly abandon something good for something even greater, even if others questioned the sanity of the endeavor. Some left doubting; others were convinced it was a good work for *someone else*, just not them.

Other helpers came for a season. They usually came to sightsee but found themselves attracted to some aspect of what we were up to. City of Refuge gave them an escape from the normalcy of life. Helping others, and investing time, talent, and treasure in an environment of real need invigorated them. Their contributions created a tremendous boost of energy and enthusiasm that benefited both the staff and the people receiving services. The folks in the season group always came to a moment of decision: "Do I fully engage my life for the benefit of others?" It was at this point that most transitioned back to a safe, normal world. Most left graciously, some just left without explanation, and a few chose to challenge the whole concept of benevolent care, arguing that the return on investment seemed less than should be expected.

The final group were those who came and stayed. The lifers. Most of them had no idea they were coming to stay; they just showed up to serve and were transformed by the work, the community, and sometimes by a single relationship. I know the profile well, because I stayed myself.

Steve Grimes is another who stayed. Honestly, when we first started talking, Steve probably thought I wasn't right in the head. Steve and I met on a retreat before I moved downtown, and some years later were invited to serve on the organizing team for another year of that same retreat. The planning meetings took place in our little church downtown, and Steve would sit by me each week and ask question after question about our organization, the work we were doing.

It was in Steve's company that I began to articulate what I meant when I said City of Refuge was devoted to benevolent care. Too often, I had heard people blame poor people for their crises, saying things like, "You don't get there without bad decisions." The implication is that they don't deserve help or second chances. Ugly stereotypes, often racially based, seem to lurk in the background of these thoughts. Forget the many obvious and real challenges to escaping crisis; the best of the poor are lazy, and the worst are criminal, is the thought.

Every day, close-up, I was learning firsthand the perilous context in which the poor operate. And the more I learned, the more I saw what others called "bad decisions" as completely rational choices given desperate, difficult circumstances. I began to believe not in second chances but thirtieth chances. Benevolent care is judgeless. And in fact, I didn't care if someone's bad decision did lead to them arriving at my door. I wouldn't ask. All I would ask is, "How can I help?"

After a few weeks of Benevolent Care 101, Steve and Linda showed up on a Sunday morning at the liquor store parking lot. Steve was originally from Oklahoma. He had never had a black friend in his life. And yet somehow, it was on that corner that he befriended Rufus. They had some kind of strange affinity and would often have each other cackling within moments of meeting. From Rufus, Steve learned how complicated—and compelled—"bad decisions" look up close.

Rufus told Steve he was twelve when he "decided" to try the crack offered to him by Miss Love, a local prostitute-turned-madam, who had shown him more care and acceptance than anyone in his life ever had. Meanwhile, so many bad decisions had already been made for Rufus, not by him. His parents had already *decided* to abandon him to his grandparents. His grandma loved him but *decided* he should drink beer at age five, "for the worms." (She believed alcohol could kill tapeworms.) His grandpa *decided* to beat him and practice voodoo rituals every time he found Rufus trying on Grandma's wig and heels. Neither of them stopped a teen-aged neighbor and then a cousin who both *decided* to molest him, though he got beatings for that, too. And Rufus himself decided to skip out on school after fourth grade.

Once-a-month visits by Steve and Linda became every other week, then every Sunday, and eventually they joined our congregation, too. Leaving their large, affluent suburban church was not nearly as difficult as they expected. Mean-while, angry, volatile, seemingly irredeemable Rufus was starting a slow transformation of his own. He was becoming a reliable guest at our parking lot meals, and before long, he was occasionally jumping on the van to church. (To this day, we've never seen someone sing gospel with such fervor.)

Then fate, as it sometimes will, forced Steve to make a decision: say goodbye, or go all in. His employer of twenty-five years notified him that they were relocating the business to another state. If Steve was going to continue to work for the company, he and Linda would have to move as well.

A lot of things weighed into Steve's decision, but among them, he knew no one else had ever stuck by Rufus. That was something he had the power to change. He quit his job, and I invited him to join our staff, which was still just a small handful strong. At that point, our budget was funded mostly by individual gifts from the congregation and from people who saw me speak in local churches and civic organizations. We also had a very small amount of foundation money. Salaries were low, and we were all just scraping by, sometimes with second jobs. We actually didn't have the money to hire Steve. His salary came from two gifts: one from his former church and one from a friend who was a successful businessman. That man continues to pay Steve's salary two decades later. Through the years, Steve has served faithfully in roles ranging from facility management to outreach coordinator to City of Refuge ambassador to other nonprofits with which we partner.

BEING "ALL IN" DOWNTOWN, keeping our doors open 24-7, we were able to get a read on where the needs were greatest in a way we never could have as part-timers. Of all the people we were meeting, it was the young women, many of them mothers, whose circumstances broke our hearts.

There was a time in my life when I would have looked at a drug-addicted, homeless mother or prostitute and seen a moral failure. From up close I saw truth quite differently. I still see a moral failure, but I don't see *her* moral failure. I can only see the myriad ways others have failed her.

So many of these women we were meeting had known

more abuse in their lives than love. They were raising children alone, the fathers MIA or in jail accused of drug-related charges, waiting months in lockup for their trials because who in 30314 can afford bail? These mothers had legal issues of their own and often needed rehab, but they were afraid that if they tried to get help, the authorities would take away their children forever.

Sara E. Jones, a 2017 summer intern to City of Refuge, summed up their reality in a column in the *Tulsa World*: "Depending on the study, between 22 percent and 57 percent of homeless women are homeless *primarily because of domestic violence. . . .* Being a woman puts a person at risk of becoming trapped in a dangerous relationship, being black puts her at risk of having nowhere to go. Systematic and institutional racism have stripped black communities of resources, and this means that black women are less likely than white women to have friends or family that are financially able to support them during in a crisis. More than 90 percent of City of Refuge's clients are black."[*]

The church where we had taken residence was also a dormitory, remember. It didn't seem so crazy, then, to start inviting some of these women and children we were meeting to live with us. We began to assume informal and sometimes

[*] Sara E. Jones, *Tulsa World,* March 25, 2018, https://www.tulsaworld.com/opinion/readersforum/sara-jones-city-of-refuge-experience-teaches-the-meaning-of/article_f6caee4a-81fa-5e7c-a397-9b7a5b776b49.html.

formal guardianship of little girls whose moms made the choice to go to rehab to address addiction issues, or to jail to resolve outstanding legal issues.

Before long, I started to get collect calls from the county jail, which wasn't far from the church. It started with a girl who was a prostitute. A john had raped her and left her on the side of the road, and she'd run down the road in nothing but her tennis shoes, knocking on people's door for help. Nobody helped, but somebody called the cops, and she ended up being arrested. When she was released, she came straight to us. Rhonda loved on her, gave her fresh clothes, and helped her get to sleep.

Soon after that, I started getting more calls from the prison. Sometimes there'd be five or six women lined up. Finally one day a lady called me and immediately started talking as if I knew her life story. "Hold on," I said. "Do we know each other?"

She answered "No."

"Well, how did you get my number?" I asked.

"Right here on the wall beside the phone! 'Need help? Call Pastor Bruce.'" Someone had written our home phone number on the wall in jail. A lot of quarters were spent calling me, and it was money well spent.

When someone finishes jail time, they're released at the same time of day they were booked. I don't know how many middle-of-the-night visits I made to pick up a woman before her pimp did. We'd have to send our daughters away from the breakfast table sometimes. The girls were so young, we didn't want them to hear the rape story or the abuse story or the prostitution story just yet. I wish I could share that every one of those stories ended in lifelong friendships and incredible success, but that would simply not be true. Trusting that someone can change their life doesn't mean you know they will—it means you believe in their ability to try, and you will do whatever you can to support them.

Valerie was the twenty-two-year-old mother of two-year-old Hannah when they came to stay with us for a while. Valerie had experienced sexual trauma at home as a child, and, since Valerie's family was still in the picture, we wanted to make sure that history did not repeat itself with Hannah. Soon Valerie got into a violent fight with her boyfriend, resulting in incarceration for both. We took paperwork to the jail and Valerie signed temporary guardianship of Hannah to Rhonda and me. Hannah settled in well and our girls loved having another playmate to roam the building with. After a few months, Valerie was released and returned to our home in the church. She was a very angry, broken person, and after a couple of situations that could have turned violent, we had to ask Valerie to move out. We restricted her ability to see Hannah. Obviously, we would not have taken such steps had the situation not been extremely volatile. Our goal was to provide a safe, caring place for Hannah and to provide mental health care and counseling for Valerie until she was ready to care for her daughter. We took small steps each day toward wholeness and reunification of their family.

Hannah flourished, but her mother continued to move in the wrong direction. She refused to get any type of help for her mental illness but continually called, wanting to come see Hannah and take her places. We had no choice but to refuse her requests.

I was sitting at my desk one day, taking care of paperwork and paying bills, when the office phone rang. I answered and Valerie told me she was outside the building and wanted to take Hannah somewhere for a couple hours. I kindly denied her request and we ended the call. Over the course of the next half an hour Valerie called multiple times, always with the same request, and I said no each time. I could sense her rising frustration but was committed to protecting the child. The final call was so over the top, I still laugh when I recall it. Valerie, in a very deliberate and measured way, said, "Pastor Bruce, if you will look out the window right now, I will point to the exact spot on my ass I want you to kiss." I looked out the window and burst out laughing. Somehow the humor made me reconsider: Was I being too overprotective, keeping mother and daughter separated? Surely I could at least let them have a chaperoned visit in the church. I invited her in to visit with Hannah. She promised that all would go smoothly and there would be absolutely no issues.

Within just a few minutes of Valerie coming into our home in the church, she was in my older daughter's bedroom, where Kassi, ten, had hung a drawing of "the Five Ks," as we had taken to calling our five daughters. Valerie was irate that Hannah wasn't in the picture and lunged to attack Kassi. Rhonda ran into the room and intervened while calling for me. I had to pick Valerie up over my shoulder and carry her to the foyer of the church. She fought me fiercely as I made my way down the steps and to the opening by the main entrance of the building. She was relentless and continued to charge at me, scratching, biting, and cursing. I had no desire to harm her and just kept pushing her away over and over.

Rhonda finally called 911 and soon after, a female Atlanta Police Department officer arrived. She subdued Valerie and placed her in cuffs. The officer interviewed me and I explained what had happened. There was a bruise on Valerie's face, she informed me. Had I struck her? I was mortified. I told her I hadn't, but I explained that it was possible Valerie had hit her face on something during our tussle. The officer then informed me that she was going to arrest both of us and let a judge determine who was at fault. Having never been arrested before, the prospect of hanging out in a holding cell did not sit particularly well with me, but I sensed that any argument with the officer would be futile. In fact, I was glad that she was being extra cautious to protect Valerie.

The officer wrote up the arrest warrant for Valerie and placed her in the back seat of the patrol car. She then wrote up my warrant and had me sign it. Just as she was preparing to cuff me, the shift supervisor for the Atlanta Police Department, who knew me and our work, walked into the church foyer. Seeing the cuffs, he immediately told the officer, "Hold up, we're not taking the preacher to jail." The officer argued a bit, then relented. I was still under arrest, the shift supervisor told me, but I was being released on my own recognizance. I'd need to head to court the next morning for a probable cause hearing. I was extraordinarily grateful, to say the least.

The next morning, after hearing the details of the case, the judge dropped all the charges. Thankfully, Valerie's charges were dropped as well, and she was released. Not too long after, we were asked to return Hannah to Valerie's family, who later moved away from the neighborhood. Rhonda and the girls cried and cried, grieving the little girl they had started to love. It was perhaps as a family our emotional awakening to the fact that we wouldn't be able to help everyone, no matter how much we loved them. Valerie was one of our first close relationships with a mother whose love vastly exceeded her capability to protect and care for her child, in large part thanks to trauma *she* experienced as a child—an incredibly difficult, complex situation that we learned we were not yet equipped to navigate. To this day, we don't know what became of either of them.

My arrest, meanwhile, had a small silver lining. Word got out quickly, and the following Sunday morning, when I walked into a sanctuary filled with many people who had been arrested and spent time in jail or prison, I was greeted by a group of folks who stood, pounded their fists on their chests, and cheered. Had I known getting arrested would give me instant street cred, I would have arranged it much earlier. To this day I have the arrest warrant in my desk drawer just in case I need to remind folks of whom they are trying to mess with.

THERE WERE SO MANY WOMEN for whom our home was a first important stop, comfortable and safe, in a long journey toward security. If I remember correctly, the largest number of people we had live with us at the same time was seventeen. With my wife, five daughters, and seventeen guests, a total of twenty-three folks were hanging out daily, sharing space and growing together. Love and a sense of possibility flowed through all those corridors that were once so gloomy and dank. There was always something to do and someone to talk to.

The name of another resident of our growing kibbutz might surprise you: Rufus. It sure surprised me. As the years passed, Steve continued to build a close relationship with Rufus and felt he needed a safe, steady place to live if he was ever to get off drugs and alcohol for good. As Steve got to know him, each new detail we learned made it easier to understand Rufus's angry, defiant lens on the world.

Miss Love, "the first one to put a spike in my arm," as Rufus will tell you, was also the first one to paint his face. He experienced it as the deepest act of loving kindness and affection he had ever known. She told him he was beautiful—and sent him on his first trick. She also gave him his new street name, Miss Choca, and his drag name, Hot Chocolate. "I was young. I was catching dates with grown mens. It was my life. It was my job. It was everything to me," he says.

When Miss Love died of AIDS, "I was the first one at her funeral." Dirty, shared needles were the norm. AIDS decimated his adoptive family in the '80s. Rufus survived because he's one of those rare people with a genetic mutation that makes him resistant to HIV. "I miss her, I miss a whole bunch of them. Straight, gays, all of 'em. I miss them all. The pimps and stuff, everybody be dyin', dyin', dyin'," he says.

Life became lonely and increasingly violent. "The time we were out there was kill or be killed. It's called survival," he says. Prostitution resulted in many physical altercations, including twice being run over by vehicles driven by customers he'd tried to rob. One of those vehicles nearly severed his leg, giving him a permanent limp. His heroin addiction and abuse of alcohol had also resulted in multiple physical issues. Rufus was legendary for his quick, violent temper, and word on the street was that Rufus had cut more folks than most surgeons had at Grady Hospital. Later he earned the name Queen Bee, and he attempted to rule the streets as royalty, ready to curse, fight, and defend his supposed turf at any time.

I wish I could say giving him a home in the basement had a sudden transformational effect, but when it came to the road to recovery, Rufus was still barely on the access ramp. No sooner than we'd give him fresh linens, clothes, and a meal, he'd disappear for days. Eventually he'd turn back up, dirty and hungry, cantankerous but briefly remorseful.

Our makeshift commune was at capacity, mostly with women, and Rufus, who identified as a man but sometimes wore dresses. Meanwhile, at the liquor store and the Street-light Café, we were feeding many men who were sleeping every night on the street. Atlanta's shelters wouldn't take them, typically because they were drunk or high. This need pointed the way to our next initiative, a lower-barrier-to-entry shelter for men. If someone could walk upright and was willing to eat a meal and go to sleep without attempting to assault anyone, they would be allowed in. Of course, we knew that even though everyone would make that commitment, we would still have those who challenged these two simple guidelines. But hey, if everything was easy, everybody would be doing it.

We rented a building almost right next to the liquor store

parking lot, on Bankhead Highway, one of the toughest streets in our city. We ordered sixty-five bed frames, mattresses, sleeping bags, and pillows. The mattresses, sleeping bags, and pillows arrived mid-December that year, but the frames were not scheduled to arrive until January. On Christmas Day the projected low temperature was twenty-three degrees. One of my staff, Philip, called and said, "Man, we gotta open the shelter for the guys. It's Christmas Day and it's freezing out." I knew he was right but I also knew we didn't have bed frames. It occurred to me that a homeless guy who is faced with the prospect of spending the night outside in twenty-three-degree weather would probably not worry too much over a bed frame.

I talked with Rhonda and, of course, she agreed that we should open the shelter. There was enough food supply in the café kitchen for me to put together a couple huge pots of chili and pack up items needed for breakfast the following morning. I kissed Rhonda and the girls and headed out. I met Philip at the building and we pulled out the mattresses and arranged them on the floor, placing a sleeping bag and pillow on each one. The little hot plate burners we brought with us took a while to get the chili piping hot again, but soon the aroma was filling the space.

We set up tables and chairs, poured drinks, and headed out into the bitter cold to find our brothers whom we had been sent to serve. Soon the building was filled with more than fifty battered souls warming themselves by the electric heaters we had plugged in around the room. We had dinner together, talked about why City of Refuge celebrates Christmas, and got ready for bed. Since opening the shelter was a last-minute decision, we didn't have staff lined up to stay the night. Philip and I realized the responsibility was now ours. Neither of us had sleeping in a shelter on our Christmas wish list, but the sacrifice felt small when we thought about the men we had just eaten with having to sleep in the cold. When the lights were turned off, we lay down on mattresses on the floor and went to sleep amid our guests. The next morning we prepared breakfast, cleaned up, and I headed back to my somewhat safe, relatively warm home. When I arrived, Rhonda asked how the night had been. I responded, "It went just fine. I slept well, all things considered." The memory of her look of disbelief still makes me laugh out loud.

The me of just a few years before could not have imagined lying down among a room full of homeless men without fear or discomfort. But now discomfort was beside the point; I was too tired and too focused. As for fear, these men had been part of my everyday life now long enough that their "otherness," while not completely erasable, barely held my notice. I slept well because, for those hours, I had stopped thinking of myself as something or someone different from the men surrounding me. Eye to eye, foot to foot, we were warm bodies who had congregated for a good meal in a warm place on a cold Christmas night.

CHAPTER 4

Life v. Death

Some people get stuck on stupid.

—L. C.

Over time, Jake's nickname for me stuck. I was now known as Ghetto Rev, but most folks just called me "Ghetto." Like most anyone with a nickname, I had no choice but to accept it—and frankly as a white guy from Virginia, I did so with pleasure. Moving downtown had changed the way I related to those we served, and them to me. Now several years in, folks were starting to believe me when I said I was with them for the long haul.

In addition to the informal care we were offering in our home, City of Refuge had also organically evolved into one of Atlanta's alternative sentencing programs. It started with a young black guy who had come to us facing time for his first drug offense. If he went to jail, he would become part of a frightening statistical reality: According to census data from 2014, there are more young black high school dropouts in prison than have jobs. One in nine black children has a parent in jail (it's one in fourteen in the general population).* It isn't hard to extrapolate the devastating social and economic effect this has on black communities.

A member of my staff went before the judge and asked if he could be released into our care instead of going to jail. We argued that he was a nonviolent offender, not a risk to others, and had a better shot at redeeming himself with us than behind bars. The judge agreed. We befriended him, fed him, sponsored him through a recovery program, made introductions that led to employment, and eventually helped him find independent housing. Periodically we began standing up like that for other people. Before long, the court started calling *us*: "The judge just sentenced this guy to your program; when can you come get him?" The crimes tended to be minor offenses such as public drunkenness, loitering, and possession, but sometimes theft. Because many of them were not first-time offenders, even petty crimes could mean serious jail time.

Occasionally we'd put up one of these individuals with us in the church basement, but more often, they were hosted by one of our volunteer families. By that point, many in our community were ready to extend the radical trust required to welcome court-ordered strangers into their homes. Over a

---

* Danielle Paquette, "One in Nine Black Children Have Had a Parent in Prison," *Washington Post*, October 27, 2015, https://www.washingtonpost.com/news/wonk/wp/2015/10/27/one-in-nine-black-children-have-had-a-parent-in-prison.

three-year period, more than a hundred men and women cycled through our program and then disappeared into private lives. At that time, we didn't have the resources to track people after they graduated. We put all our focus on doing everything we could while they were in our care to give them a shot at staying out of prison and building a stable life.

Meanwhile, we had a growing circle of people who had been with us since the beginning. Jake was working on overcoming his crack addiction, and he had a steady job for the first time in many years. Now off the streets, he was living in a home operated by one of the folks who came to stay. He seemed to be doing exceptionally well and was named house manager and given extra responsibility and privileges. My girls loved Jake and he loved them. He would show up for a church service or event, and with a big grin on his weathered face, he would hug the girls tight. Then he'd look from them to me, and say something like, "Don't know how y'all make it with Ghetto as your daddy. Thank God you got Mama Rhonda." He and I would talk about golf and he would give me a tip here and there when we played. When my swing inevitably failed to improve (I'm arguably beyond instruction), he'd smirk and say, "Ghetto, you sure are hardheaded. I could make you a great golfer, but you never gonna listen." He had a well-aimed sarcasm that got me every time.

Sober and clean Jake was friendly, outgoing, and cared a lot for others. His interest felt all the more genuine because he had no facade. Those he didn't like knew it. He couldn't stand Rufus. "Why you still feeding him, Ghetto?" he'd ask, with real frustration. "Why you keep puttin' clothes on his back, when he do nothin' but hate on everybody?"

Then, without warning, Jake left. The transitional house he was staying in had a six o'clock curfew, and when the supervisor arrived at home that evening around nine, Jake wasn't there. His belongings were still in his room, but he had simply walked away without a word to anyone. When the supervisor called me, I immediately knew where Jake had gone—and I knew I would have to go get him before it was too late.

BY THAT TIME, I had started to piece together the details of Jake's life. He didn't like to talk about his past, but sometimes details would slip out, usually when he was drinking. I was aching to know how it was that the same man who could join me at the fancy private golf course and make amiable conversation with well-to-do strangers was also the man I had met on a feeding line.

"Jake" turned out to be the name he had given himself. (He was a fan of Westerns, which had a lot of Jakes.) His parents had named him Ernest. They were sharecroppers on a former cotton plantation. His father was short of temper and violent, quick to beat him and his mother. One of Jake's earliest memories was his mother locking them in a closet while his father shot at the door.

Young Jake ran away from home for days at a time, camping out in the woods alone at a younger age than most kids these days would be allowed to walk to the bus stop. There are so many questions about that period in his life that I wish I had answers to: How did he feed himself? Did he ever get sick? Was he lonely? How long did he go to school? Did teachers try to help him?

He might have ended up making a living in the fields, except that at some point in his early teens he camped next to a public golf course and took an interest in the game. I guess he talked his way into caddying and practice time—not too hard to imagine. Jake could charm a snake. By the time I met him, he was the Westside's best, possibly only, homeless semipro golfer. He had made good money that way over the years, alternatively hustling or giving lessons, depending on what opportunity the day offered. He also took work as a landscaper, always under the table. He had a group of guys in the neighborhood whom he was friendly with, but he was mostly a loner.

The time line is fuzzy. He married a minister and had a daughter with her. When he was thirty-six, he was found guilty of commercial gambling—a felony conviction for activities that in many other parts of our country, carried out by other people, are considered acceptable business transactions.

(Vegas, anyone?) Becoming a felon probably ruined any chances of him settling into a more normal life. When you can't vote and, as far as most employers are concerned, you can't work, you're in trouble.

In Jake's forties, by his telling, drink got the best of him. His marriage fell apart and he never reconciled with his wife or daughter. Then came crack and life on the streets. So that's where he was when we met, in his early fifties. On his good days, he was a friend and comrade in arms. On his bad days, forget it—a wrong look and he would explode in anger, sometimes violently. I don't know what his medical diagnosis was, but it seemed like he was bipolar, with crack and alcohol tied into the swings. I don't know which was the chicken or which the egg. (A very high percentage of people who suffer from bipolar disorder also struggle with addiction to alcohol and drugs.*)

The winter night I set off after Jake was cold, and darkness seemed to overwhelm the streetlights as I parked my car in The Bluff, then one of the nation's most notorious open-air drug markets. Jake's traditional turf for scoring crack was an area of about half a dozen blocks. I got out and started wandering the streets, looking for my friend. Block after block, no Jake, just my own mounting despair. Then I remembered

---

* Michael G. Pipich, "The Bipolar-addiction Connection," *Psychology Today,* September 10, 2018, https://www.psychologytoday.com/us/blog/owning-bipolar/201809/the-bipolar-addiction-connection.

that Jake would sometimes go to the Lotto shop on Bankhead Highway and clean up for his cousin who ran the place.

Now, everyone knew that a lot more than unlimited Lotto tickets was sold at that shop, but I guess law enforcement turned a blind eye. The place had ten or so small tables where people would sit to eat and gamble. It took me a couple minutes to talk myself into entering the establishment, where I knew I might not receive the warmest of welcomes. I reminded myself that Jake was likely in the shop. He was my friend and I believed I could talk him off the ledge. The internal pep talk led me to the doorstep, and sheer will convinced me to step inside. People were wall to wall in the shop, every table taken, and a standing-room-only crowd was assembled. Various groups were throwing dice and playing cards, and the smell of weed and crack cocaine permeated the air.

Through a thick haze, I saw Jake with a broom on the other side of the room; he was still cleaning, so I knew he hadn't yet earned his bag of rock. My entrance was something like you see in the movies—activity ground to a halt and all eyes shifted to me. My clothing was nothing to attract attention. My skin color was another story. Conversation ceased midsentence, and where seconds before the space had been filled with laughing, singing, cursing, and conversation, now the room was dead silent. I stood just inside the door, the object of everyone's attention. I did not move and I did not speak. I just stood. In what seemed to be slow motion,

Jake dropped his broom and moved through the crowd of people with a look of great alarm on his face. Coming within inches of my face, Jake whispered with urgency, "You can't be in here, Ghetto, they will kill you, Ghetto."

"Who will kill me, Jake?" I asked.

"These people in this room will kill you," he answered with a depth of sincerity that caused me to begin to worry a bit more than previously.

"Why, Jake?"

"Ghetto," Jake breathed, "you're white, that's why. You don't belong here and they don't want you here. By the way, Ghetto, why *are* you here?"

Looking Jake in the eyes, I told him that I was there for him, to take him back to the house where his things were, to help him. It was a quick conversation, but Jake didn't take long to decide he'd come with me. He stepped into the back room, and for an uneasy moment I felt alone in the cold intensity of so many hostile eyes. Moments later he was back with his jacket, and we backed out the door and moved quickly down the sidewalk without looking back.

Jake trusted me enough—or cared enough about my safety—to walk out the door by my side.

That night I was relieved, but it felt like too close a call. If I hadn't found Jake, would he have ever come back? The near relapse seemed to call into question not just Jake's progress but also the question of whether anyone could change. By that point I had seen so many people who, at the deepest levels of desperation, though their decisions had led them to hell and back, had no interest in listening to the counsel of others. It was hard to interact with these folks without bringing shame and blame into the conversation, and honestly, there were still times my staff—with me, no doubt, as their model—laced their counsel with this negative attitude. We then made things worse by setting the bar for transformation impossibly high. The vision of a sober life of independence and responsibility to others was so far away from people's reality that they received the vision more like a blur.

In school, I had been trained to create processes and programs that would lead to certain outcomes—something like a business model with a biblical flavor. People would come and you would plug them into one of the programs or the processes, and they would move from point A to point B to point C, transformed. The training I'd had made sense when everybody in the room looked the same, sounded the same, and came from the same background, or when the "problems" we were chewing on were theoretical or petty grievances that made spoiled Christians uncomfortable.

Here? No one looked like me, no one sounded like me, and the problems they had were the opposite of theoretical. Pushing people to conform to my agenda, or align with my personal standards of behavior, didn't seem appropriate. I couldn't say, "I trust you, let's be friends" and then turn around and immediately tell someone the "right" way to live. If someone wanted to make a change, both the initiative and the direction needed to come from them. I wrestled internally and often argued with myself regarding the best path forward.

Meanwhile, we were still feeding many of the same folks that we had fed every week in the parking lot since our first days. We were sharing clothing and blankets with some of the same friends we shared clothing and blankets with last year. Of course there were success stories along the way and really powerful life transformations took place now and then, but compared to the number of "not yet" stories, the return on our investment didn't seemed all that impressive. Worrying about our slow rate of progress often led me to spirals of seemingly unanswerable doubt about whether we were doing the right work in the right way.

By this point, it wasn't just Jake saying we should discontinue our care for Rufus. I had staff members requesting it, too. They had legitimate reasons. He was ungrateful, obnoxious, rude, and hateful. He fussed about the food we served. He complained that the coat we gave him wasn't the right color. He didn't want to be picked up at the time we arranged to take him for medical appointments. He was fickle with his preferences, yet any failure to satisfy them was met with great personal offense. Deep within him was the belief that others were there to take him down, not build him up, which led to him constantly orienting himself away from the help he needed. We offered him a home; he chose the cold hard ground. We offered addiction recovery programs; he chose the crack pipe and heroin needle. We offered friendship; he chose to push everyone away. Again and again, we came back. And again and again, Rufus told us to go away.

And yet I couldn't give up. I knew the circumstances that had hardened him to such a sharp, unstable point. And inevitably, anytime I reached a low moment of thinking his case was hopeless, he'd shake me with some new revelation.

A great example was when we learned that, against all odds, Rufus had a second, on-and-off, occupation. He told us he had trained in Florida as a nursing assistant and passed "with flyin' colors" an exam for a certificate that allowed him to work in nursing homes, caring for the elderly and incapacitated—"taking care of them, loving on them," as he describes it. The fact that he had pursued, acquired, and taken clear pleasure in such work was a reminder that no one is merely a victim, even of the worst circumstances.

In the first few years I knew Rufus, he'd get one of these jobs now and then, but his tenure would always be remarkably short. Either his addiction would get in the way of his performance, or he'd curse out a supervisor if they said anything critical. Rufus hated for folks to "shine on him," by which he meant calling him out or disciplining him in front of others. He despised anyone trying to tell him how to live his life. Rufus's characterization of such interlopers was often stated as follows: "Dey all up in my Kool-Aid and dey don't even know the flavor." His anger ran deep and his resentment toward those he perceived as against him (at some point, everybody) ran even deeper. Radical emotions would often boil over like water in an unwatched pot, scalding those nearest him.

ONE NIGHT, during the height of my period of worry about Jake and the more general dearth of transformation we'd so far witnessed, relief came from an unlikely source. I was sitting next to a fresh fire in the chilly darkness outside of our home. At this time, we were inviting people to weekly nighttime hot dog roasts. We'd pass out wire hangers, and pile all the trimmings on a table at the edge of the yard. A couple dozen chairs were set up in a circle, most of them occupied by guys from the street. A lot of people think of homelessness as a lifetime occupation. Yet sitting around those fires were not just men whose lives never got footing but also formerly successful businessmen, husbands, and fathers—men who had built lives that, at some point, were laid to ruin, most often by substance abuse but also by the kind of run of bad luck that only ends in homelessness when you're already poor. Now these men were grateful to sit beside a fire eating hot dogs and chips and drinking soda provided by City of Refuge.

(These days the food we serve is generally more nutritious, but there will always be something special about roasting hot dogs by the fire.) Everyone knew that singing would follow, a devotional would be given, and prayer would be offered for those who desired it. Most of the guys had very little interest in the song, the devotion, or the prayer, but they would linger and tolerate it out of respect and gratitude to those who brought the food.

I was sitting beside L. C., an ex-con, on-and-off-again addict, semifunctional alcoholic, whom I first met when he was among a handful of men living in a graveyard off Cleveland Avenue. Graveyards are a pretty good deal when you're homeless—soft grass, tree cover, and for the most part, you're left alone, other than when they need to mow the grass or bury someone. I'd had one guy from the graveyard show up in my office telling me, "God mowed my dope." It turned out the mower had plowed right through his stash, next to a headstone, and he took it as a sign it was time to get his life in order.

As for L. C., he'd move to a shelter during cold weather. From there he would enter a recovery program about once a year, where he'd stay awhile, transition to his own little apartment, crash and burn, and the vicious cycle would begin again. On this particular evening, L. C. was living in one of our transitional-living houses. L. C. was the only name he would share with us, even though we had known him for a number of years. We talked a bit about stuff that guys talk about when they are sitting around a fire in the yard: weather, sports, and thoughts on the current state of politics.

L. C.'s vocabulary was varied and his insights were thoughtful. He often pondered prior to speaking, measuring his words to deliver greatest impact. Yet his hard living meant he would lose track now and then and the path of the conversations would take multiple detours along the way. There were no brief conversations with L. C., and one needed to concentrate intently to follow the path of discourse. There were times I walked away from him thinking, *Well, there's fifteen minutes of my life I'll never get back.* But L. C. was our friend, and on this night he wanted to talk, and I was glad to listen. All around the circle, people were chatting quietly among one another.

After a while our conversation turned to more serious topics. L. C. related a couple prison stories so violent they made my skin crawl. All those hardships seemed to have been mapped into in the deep lines of his fifty-year-old face. At one point, L. C. looked around cautiously, lowered his voice, and confided, "You know there are dead bodies in my past." I shuddered inside, but I understood that he didn't want to hold anything back. I kindly asked him not to share the details that night, and he nodded slightly. In his husky, southern, somewhat resigned voice, L. C. told me of moving from place to place, stealing to buy drugs, struggling to stay warm, fighting his addictions daily, and losing regularly. He also told me about seasons of freedom and sobriety and a level of normalcy he experienced now and then.

Without realizing it, L. C. was bringing to the surface all the frustration I'd felt in recent weeks. By now, I knew well the social and economic factors that were working against folks, not to mention the physical compulsion of addiction. Yet I wasn't ready to throw personal agency entirely out the window. "What's the deal, L. C.? Can you explain to me how someone chooses behavior that leads to destruction, decides to change that behavior, reverts back, spends time in prison, is beaten and left for dead, starts over, falls down, and the cycle repeats itself over and over and over?"

My question hung in the air. We found ourselves in one of L. C.'s moments of pondering. But this one lasted a very long time, uncomfortably long. L. C. had his eyes closed and seemed to have moved to another place altogether. I was convinced that I had either offended or angered him, and I deeply hoped that was not the case. I understood that things could quickly turn dark in his mind, and I had little desire to get into a physical altercation with this veteran of the streets. His prison stories had thrown me. Eventually, L. C. exhaled deeply, opened his eyes, and turned to look me in the face.

"Ghetto, some people just get stuck on stupid."

I didn't show up that night expecting to advance my education. I have a degree in biblical education with an emphasis on pastoral studies from a university with a great reputation in the traditional theological arena. I have sat before great minds and listened to lectures on ethics, morality, life choices, social issues, and the like. I have read extensively regarding the impact of trauma, addictive tendencies, and personality disorders. Yet here, next to a parking lot fire, sitting on a folding chair, I received a new angle on the truth.

Now it was my turn to ponder. L. C. seemed to be saying there would be some people I could never help—they'd stay stuck on stupid. It was their choice and they'd keep making it. It was out of my hands. In a selfish sense, this was incredibly liberating. Giving up the messiah complex—the belief that we have to save everyone in trouble—was a wonderful, cathartic experience, and a necessary one. My calling was to serve people in crisis, not make judgments or demands. Imposing a dynamic of "savior and saved" wasn't good for anyone, nor was it accurate. Take excessive drinking. There was a time I might have approached a binge drinker with the assumption that alcohol was the vice that lead him to ruin. Sometimes, it was; but just as often drinking was a coping mechanism, a rational response to impossible circumstances. And until I could give someone a home and a practical path forward, how could I see booze as anything but self-medication, a way to survive brutal, painful days and nights?

Very clearly I could see places in my own life where I, too, had been stuck on stupid. Part of the reason why drug paraphernalia in the offering plate didn't send me running was that I had seen it up close and personal before. I went to high school and college in the late '70s; alcohol and drug use were prevalent, and the circles I ran in were no different. I personally drank to excess, smoked a good bit of weed, and even tried speed—the last of which proved to be a poor companion to the intense temper I was known for in my youth. In that period, I had many experiences that led me to places of extreme pain and confusion, yet not to any immediate change in behavior. The gate of my blocked memory bank opened wide, and scene after scene of "stupid" flashed by on the screen. It was a wonderful, freeing experience to stop blaming others, stop blaming circumstances, stop deflecting, and just accept responsibility for my own times of unintelligent, foolish behavior. It was also sobering. To commit fully to helping others, I would have to accept that many people would never be saved, not by me, not by themselves, or by anyone else.

LATER THAT WEEK, I sat quietly in the sanctuary, thinking about L. C.'s words and how they reflected on the message of encouragement I wanted to deliver to a house full of brave souls Sunday morning. I thought about the Israelite leader Joshua. L. C. offered only one option, getting stuck on stupid. Joshua, however, offered two options when he said, "Today you get to choose life or death, blessing or cursing." Joshua believed every day brought a new opportunity to get unstuck. I guess he had never sat around a firepit eating weenies with someone like L. C.

I had spent most of my life thinking, like Joshua, that the choice to get unstuck was equally simple for everyone. I started to think about why I myself hadn't stayed stuck on stupid. There were always so many forces pulling me back—resources of family, community, and education that all added up to believing in the best version of myself, not the worst. In many ways doing good was the path of least resistance. I also had enough self-esteem to admit failure and not have it define me.

L. C. and so many others we worked with didn't have any of those things to draw strength from. There was no family support system. He didn't have an education or a clear vision of a better future. All he had was his addiction.

If circumstances tilt the scale dramatically toward one result, what was the best way to support people like L. C.? I couldn't undo the life he had lived, nor could I fight his battle for him. What I *could* do was light up his future path with dignity in the present. Not only was it the ethical thing to do, it was also the best way to support him.

And if he never made good choices? It was still the right thing to do, and I would no longer beat myself up about it.

I stopped seeing any utility in carping on or even discussing the decisions people had already made. Periodically, I make the statement, "It is what it is." My wife dislikes that attitude greatly, but in the case of City of Refuge and the people we were serving, it seemed to resonate. *It is what it is—* now let's look forward to the next moment and agree that it will be different. Life had already served L. C. and our other friends a suffocating heap of recrimination and judgment, so we knew that approach had had zero success. My approach was untested, but surely it could beat that abysmal track record. Our contribution would always be one of encouragement, whether we were meeting someone in the Streetlight Café or on the street outside the jail after his or her release.

I had flung a mental door open, and light now flooded the room. I sat down with my staff and volunteers, and we recommitted to starting every day of every relationship with a blank slate, focused not on the endgame but on now—the decisions and actions that made each day better than the one before. In my sermon that week, and going forward, I stopped talking about the negative effect of bad choices. Instead I looked out into the room and shared stories that emphasized the positive effect of good choices, even in the face of obstacles. Seeing one face after another light up with hope, I knew this was a powerful shift.

As a result of my personal enlightenment, our relationships with Jake, Rufus, and others began to take on a different approach. We checked ourselves against shaming and blaming. We stopped thinking about and talking about changing their lives forever. Rather, we worked to help them make one choice at a time to bring a little positive change to their lives. Getting through a day without Jake running away was now counted a success. Having a dinner service take place at the liquor store parking lot without Rufus tossing a pan of green beans at a volunteer was now counted a success. It was a huge success to see Gloria only slightly stumbling rather than falling down drunk. The shift in approach took hold easily among the staff because the returns were immediately observable, and we made a habit of celebrating each one.

Over the next few months we gathered as usual on Sunday mornings in our little church, now more than half full every week. Folks in need sat side by side with folks who wanted to help. I started to witness many of our friends who had been fighting losing battles begin to win a few skirmishes along the way. For some, daily drug abuse was reduced to just a few times a week. Outbursts of anger and violence became less often and more subdued. A willingness to accept advice was more prevalent. Gratitude replaced suspicion in some, a shift that seemed to be contagious. I noticed that when the leader of a small group of our friends began to demonstrate more of a spirit of gratitude, others followed quickly.

You might have heard the rule of thumb that a drug craving passes in nine minutes. Recently one of the women in House of Cherith, our sex-trafficking recovery program—a part of our journey that you'll hear about later—was packing her bags to leave. She was a heroin addict and wanted out. So we sat down with her on the floor. I took her hands and held them gently. "I don't need you to tell me you'll be clean tomorrow," I said. "I need you to sit here with me for nine minutes. Let's get through nine more minutes together." We counted down, several times, and eventually she decided she could hang in another day.

Not every case involves a countdown, but nine-minute increments is a good metaphor for how I changed my approach in those months after my fireside chat with L. C. We weren't there to save the world, or even an individual in it. We were there to hold hands, in nine-minute increments, as many as were needed.

Section Two

CHAPTER 5

The One Stop Shop

Mercy is a force that compels us to acts of compassion.
But in time mercy will collide with an ominous,
opposing force. Injustice.

—ROBERT D. LUPTON[*]

H ere's a scenario that I'm guessing every person reading this book has faced, no matter where you live. A man on the street corner asks you for a dollar. Maybe he says it's for food, maybe he doesn't. In barely a second, you take in information about him—dirty tattered clothes, maybe no shoes, maybe signs of health troubles or substance abuse— and start calculating the advisability of giving him your money. Do you respond to his clear need without caring about consequences? Decline to give him money but buy him a sandwich? Ignore him completely but make a mental note

---

[*] Robert D. Lupton, *Toxic Charity: How the Church Hurts Those They Help and How to Reverse It* (New York: HarperOne, 2011), 40.

to contribute to an organization—maybe one like mine—who might give him tools for real transformation?

If you've ever been on that street corner running through your options, you have some idea of what I was facing at the helm of a growing benevolent-care organization. My initial commitment to Rhonda that we would live in the church for only a year had long ago been forgotten. We were somehow, suddenly, in our sixth year. Our after-school and camping programs for children and youth were in full operation. The food and clothing outreaches to those in need were continuing apace. The men's shelter now had sixty-five bed frames to go with the mattresses and was full most nights. The little building we lived in was completely utilized, with classrooms being used as living quarters for single mothers and their children, the café serving hundreds of meals weekly, and gatherings of all kinds taking place in the sanctuary. More people than we could count had lived in the building with us, eaten at our table, received our trust and care, and been provided with resources to help them on their journey to stability. The language of transformation had been replaced by the celebration of small steps.

We had learned and accomplished a lot. And then came a disturbing event that, in retrospect, proved to be an important inflection point in the evolution of City of Refuge.

A man named Michael was a resident in our men's shelter. We knew very little about him, only that he was homeless and suffered from mental illness. He had complied with all the guidelines in terms of rules and behavior. That changed suddenly one night when he walked up to the overnight staff person and dropped his pants, demanding the person put ointment on the open sores on his genitalia. The staff member refused, and Michael reacted with such an explosion of anger that he had to be physically removed from the building. When Chris, the overnight supervisor, exited the building the next morning he found that Michael had climbed onto the hood of Chris's truck and defecated on the windshield. While quite unappealing and very nasty, the rest of us got a great laugh out of Chris's dilemma. As Rhonda has said, "Compassion sometimes has an odor." Humor was the way we got through those moments.

A couple of days after the truck incident, I was checking voice mails in the office and Michael had left the most profane message I've ever heard. There were combinations of curse words I had never heard, along with suggestions of things I should do that I am pretty sure are impossible. I laughed again and decided it was good enough to keep in my voice mailbox for a while. (It always makes me laugh when people think profanity is the best way to offend a pastor. I hear more profanity and vulgar language in a week in the streets than most folks hear in a year, so someone like Michael trying to shock me was always funny.)

A couple of weeks later Michael walked into my office and

asked to be allowed to return to the shelter. In mild shock, I asked him why he should be allowed back after his vulgar voice mail, not to mention his smelly signature on Chris's truck. He hadn't apologized or asked forgiveness for his behavior. His response was, "I didn't shit on Chris's truck and I never left any messages." I pushed the play button on my phone and let Michael listen to the voice mail. He laughed and said, "That's not me. That's someone imitating my voice. You know, I think that's Rich Little pretending to be me." (Rich Little, for those who are too young to remember, is an impersonator who used to do Johnny Carson's *Tonight Show* and a lot of other TV talk and variety shows, primarily during the '60s and '70s.)

I told Michael that I couldn't let him back in the shelter and that he should move along pretty quickly. He stormed out of my office, slamming the exit door loudly. I could hear him shouting as he walked through the parking lot. Moments later, one of the team burst into my office and yelled, "Michael's trying to kill Raymond!"

Sprinting into the parking lot, I discovered Michael waving a cinder block in front of Raymond's face and telling him that he did, indeed, intend to kill him. I didn't think. I walked between the two men, looked Michael in the eyes, and told him that he was not going to hurt Raymond or anyone else. He was going to drop the cinder block then and there. With as dark a look as I recall ever seeing from anyone, Michael dropped the cinder block and in a deep, guttural voice I'd never heard from him before, said, "I'll be back to kill you and Rhonda and your girls. I know when Rhonda leaves in the morning taking the girls to school, and I know when she gets home. I'll be back soon and you all are going to die."

With that, he turned and strode down the street. The threat felt serious and imminent. I called the cops. A patrolman arrived soon thereafter, and I shared the story with him. As we were talking, Michael walked around the building and headed straight toward me, declaring again his intention to kill my entire family. The officer immediately arrested Michael and took him away.

A few days later I was once again in Superior Court, this time in a probable cause hearing where the judge would determine if there was enough evidence of threat to bind Michael over to a trial at a later date. After I sat through several hearings, the clerk called me to the front of the courtroom, where I stood just a few feet from the judge. A deputy was stationed on my left side and Michael entered the courtroom on my right side, cuffed and with a deputy on either side of him. The deputies escorted Michael to within just a few feet of me, facing the judge as well. Before the judge could speak, Michael turned toward me, pointed his finger in my direction as though it were a gun, and with a shooting motion, simply said, "Pow." As deputies grabbed him by the arms, the judge spoke decisively: "We're gonna keep him," he said, and they ushered him out quickly.

IN SIX YEARS, there had been many days of frustration, moments of anger and snippets of time when I thought exhaustion might overtake me. Rhonda and I were parenting five daughters and raising money daily to survive, and we were steadfastly sitting on the sidewalk with the alcoholic as he or she threw up the poison consumed the previous night. We were serving as guardians for little girls, housing their moms, trying to find safe, affordable places for them to go. But even on the hardest days, in those moments when nothing seemed to be working, I had always been able to make a conscious decision to press on, do more, give extra, love even more deeply.

The episode with Michael shook me to my core. Now, for the first time, I felt unsure. Having our lives threatened by a mentally ill man was a whole new level of difficult. It was the first time I had ever been concerned for my family's wellbeing. Sure, I'd had moments in the past where I felt conflicted about the impact of our work on our family. By uprooting them from our quiet life in the suburbs, was I doing them a disservice? Was I exposing them to too much of the dirty, grimy, desperate side of life? Rhonda and I both believed in what we were doing, but neither of us had ever truly thought we were putting our daughters at risk.

The episode with Michael made that feel like a real possibility. Plenty of days it was hard to tell if I was succeeding or what the impact was. Was this worth putting my and my family's lives at stake?

Some three weeks after Michael's arrest, I found myself back in the same courtroom, this time seated near the front as the court-appointed psychiatrist read the results from his interviews with Michael. The reports made it clear that Michael had multiple mental health issues and was often delusional. At times he would recall being a bodyguard for Elvis Presley. Other times he told stories of when he was the Green Hornet and had his own television show. In an attempt to determine if Michael understood right from wrong, the psychiatrist asked Michael if he was aware that, if released, harming my family or me would be wrong. Michael replied that yes, he knew it would be wrong. Following up, the psychiatrist asked, "If the judge releases you, what do you intend to do?" With great sincerity Michael answered, "I intend to hunt the son of a bitch down and shoot his ass." Once the laughter in the courtroom had died down, the judge sentenced Michael to incarceration and additional mental health evaluation with his release date to be determined by the mental health specialist at a future time.

I was relieved, deeply relieved. Michael couldn't hurt

anyone outside the mental health facility. But I was also troubled. If I hadn't thrown him out of the shelter, might things have ended differently? Maybe we could have gotten him the psychiatric help he needed. Instead he had become one more mentally ill person now receiving the "care" of the criminal justice system. Michael ultimately spent three years in jail. Three years later after he was finally released, I saw him on the street one day. I felt myself tense in alarm, until his eyes passed over me, vacant. He shuffled on by, having completely forgotten who I was.

I left the courtroom that day with a pit in my stomach. Michael had put the period on a sentence I had been meditating on for some time. City of Refuge needed to do more, be more. The crisis triage and resource matching we were providing felt woefully inadequate to problems of the people we met; since Michael, I was back to feeling like the suburbanite handing out bologna sandwiches. Crisis triage was important to building relationships but insufficient on its own. Of course, we were also connecting as many people as we could with resources to help them make their next steps. We referred people to mental health services, addiction recovery programs, free legal help, whatever they needed. The services were out there. But the people we were working with were fighting so many battles that they often failed to follow through. Coming to us had been hard enough. Now we were asking them to connect with three or four different agencies, none of whom communicated with one another in a meaningful way. Atlanta is a sprawling city, making it very difficult for people without their own reliable car or money to get themselves where they need to go, especially on someone else's timetable. Add to that the hassle and humiliations of bureaucracy, and their getting help on their own seems impossible. I was afraid that the resources we were handing out were the charitable equivalent of pouring water in front of a thirsty person without giving them a cup.

Then there was another question: Was a lifetime devoted to crisis triage sustainable, for me or anyone else who had committed to our journey?

I had met people who set out to do good and who had become callous or unfeeling along the way. Bitterness could be heard in their voices and frustration seemed to be a constant companion, because the objects—a carefully chosen word—of their compassion had in some way failed their expectation. I was a long way from there, but you could say the experience with Michael had knocked the bloom off the rose, at least temporarily. I didn't like the frustration I admittedly felt when someone in our care fell back into destructive behaviors, especially when I sensed the help we could provide was so inadequate.

One hot and muggy summer day, an exchange with a

stranger forced me to reflect on where I might be heading if we didn't expand our vision at City of Refuge. It seems all my personal revelations take place in parking lots, and this time it was in the one behind our church home. I was there cleaning up when a guy from the street whom I had not met before walked up. As I placed trash in the back of my truck he walked over and leaned against the truck and said hello. I responded without showing much interest and moved back to the task at hand. One more homeless guy walking up wasn't enough to cause me to alter my plans. I was busy.

Looking in the bed of the truck, the guy noticed an old pair of running shoes that I would wear in to work from time to time. The shoes had a lot of miles on them and wouldn't ordinarily be something a person would desire—unless, of course, the shoes the person was wearing were in even worse condition. Turning his gaze to me, he made his request. "Mind if have those shoes?" It was an easy yes. I had plenty of shoes and this particular pair held no sentimental value, not to mention the fact that they had been rained on, sweated in, and left in a truck bed for months.

"Sure, you can have them," I replied.

Reaching into the truck bed, he picked up the shoes, took a long look at them, and placed them on the tailgate, where he also sat down. He untied his worn shoes with visible holes in the soles, removed them, and dropped them to the asphalt parking lot as though they were contagious and he wanted nothing more to do with them. I turned back to my work and he sat in silence for a few moments. "Excuse me," I heard him say, and as I turned toward him he continued, "Would you happen to have a pair of socks I could have?" Only then did I notice he was barefoot and had not been wearing socks under his shoes.

"Of course, let me get you some," I replied, and quickly went upstairs. I opened the drawer where I kept my socks and from more than two dozen I picked out a pair for him. Back outside, the man was still seated on the tailgate of my truck. He accepted the socks with gratitude. In the sun they seemed blindingly white. He didn't move to put them on his feet. He just sat there holding them in his hand, head down. Sensing that he wanted to say something else, I stood and waited quietly.

After a few uncomfortable moments of silence he looked up and softly asked, "Any chance I could wash my feet?"

Some moments get seared into your mind like hot brands into the tough hide of cattle. There is an immediate painful experience that you will never forget, but beyond that, something new is now a part of you. The look on his face and the words that he spoke were branded to my soul and I will always live with them. I was struck by the shame and embarrassment his eyes revealed as he made his request. His voice seemed to quiver as he forced the words out. The man, my new friend, exerted enormous energy in his simple request to wash his feet. I felt the impact deeply. His bravery in that moment made me hot with shame for the apathy I felt when he first approached. *Too busy to interrupt my day for one more homeless guy.*

He followed me into the basement of the church where I showed him the way to the bathroom, provided him with a towel, washcloth, and the items he would need to not only wash his feet but also take a shower. I quickly looked through my closet and pulled out underwear, a shirt, and pants that looked like they would fit. I placed them on the counter outside the shower room and left a trash bag for him to toss his old clothes in.

A full half hour passed as he stood under the hot water, scrubbed his head and body, and shaved several weeks of stubble from his face. I spent each of those minutes deep in recrimination. I wondered why I was frustrated when the guy walked onto the property and interrupted my plans for the day. I wondered why I didn't notice his worn-out shoes and offer replacements before he had to ask. How had I not been aware that he didn't have socks? Why had I almost shut myself off from the opportunity to help someone experience the satisfaction of being clean, groomed, and well-clothed again, even if just for a day or two?

Sitting there I realized that even doing good was not enough if the doing became ritual, rote, or routine. Or worse, if doing good started to feel like an interruption to "more important work," like cleaning out my car. My initial reluctance to meet this man's needs scared me and scarred me. I promised myself that I would not have to be branded in this way again.

BETWEEN THAT EXPERIENCE and Michael's threats and incarceration, my wheels were churning on the question of the path forward for City of Refuge. No longer could I be satisfied hoping that the haphazard resources and referrals we were providing would change anyone's life. As we were an organization, it was time to offer longer-term, more complete solutions.

I began to imagine something I came to call the One Stop Shop: an array of services that would give individuals in crisis every possible resource they might need on their journey to independence, all under one roof. We would have doctors and therapists, addiction recovery programs, job training and placement, day cares, and schools. These wraparound services, offered in one residential location, would allow the people we served a dedicated and safe space to make their recovery. Some of the service organizations might be autonomous partners, but they would work together closely so that every treatment program was completely holistic.

If we wanted a one-stop shop, we were going to have to build it from the ground up. It simply didn't exist yet among Atlanta's social service providers, at least as far as I knew.

And if we were going to build it, we needed more space. We were still operating out of our home in the church, which was at capacity at twenty-three. There was no room for growth.

I asked a friend in the real estate business to go deeper into the highest-need neighborhoods and find us a building. Our initial location had many challenges but paled in comparison to the area surrounding The Bluff, the place I felt we were now supposed to go. Historical data indicated that the zip code I felt we needed to relocate to had, per capita, the highest crime rate in the state, the highest homeless population, more men and women incarcerated from that zip code than from any other in the state. Statistics showed 73 percent of the children lived in single-adult homes and 33 percent lived two and a half times below the poverty level. Abandoned homes and boarded-up apartments littered the community and gang activity was rampant.

Even before a building had been identified, people who had been with us for all or most of the six years told me they would not be going with us if we moved there. The neighborhood, in their eyes, was so dangerous, so far from redemption, that they didn't want anything to do with it. Perhaps I should not have been surprised, but I was. These people had been crucial in building our community. They knew firsthand what good work done well could accomplish, but now that the stakes were elevating, the desire to live safe and protected lives overrode the desire to make sure others could simply live. The resentment and disdain I felt for some of those who chose to leave has long since faded away. In hindsight I realize they were there for their season, and even though I think some of them should have stayed, I've come to a place of understanding that it's not up to me to determine someone else's destiny. Each of us must work it out for ourselves.

My real estate buddy, Rick, called me one day, excited. He had found a property that seemed to be just what I was looking for. "Eight acres of land, with five acres of warehouse under roof," he said, "with an eight-foot fence with razor wire and an armed guard at the gate, right in the middle of the hood." My response was, "Sounds like a dream come true—now find out how much they want for it."

Rick called a few days later and informed me the owner was asking $1.6 million for the property and building. One point six million dollars! Not being the greatest of negotiators, my counteroffer was, "We don't have any money." Not surprisingly, the owner turned down my generous offer but he did agree to meet and get to know about the work we intended to do in the community in case our position improved.

Over the next few months, the owner, Malon Mimms, and I became friends. At seventy-one, Malon had a long and successful career in commercial real estate. He was down-to-earth, sharp, and engaging. We hit it off immediately. Sitting across from him over a number of sessions, I shared the vision I had for City of Refuge, the one-stop shop.

Malon was listening, I could tell. But ultimately he would smile and nod, and I would leave with no indication that the price of the building would be lowered anytime soon. Something compelled me to continue showing up at his office to have lunch and talk, so I did.

FINALLY, I got a call from Rick. A staffer from Malon's office had just called him, asking how soon City of Refuge could close on the property located at 1300 Joseph Boone Boulevard in Atlanta. Rick's immediate response was total confusion. He informed the individual that we still didn't have any money. "We know," the staff person answered. "Malon wants to donate the property and would like to close as soon as possible." We were shocked and elated. The news seemed like providential confirmation that we were on the right path.

The donation took place in August 2003. Obviously, we had never owned a fifty-year-old, 210,000-square-foot warehouse in the hood, and while I had made some big statements about what we would do if we had the property, I was now faced with having to figure out what we really would do now that it had miraculously become ours.

The donated building quickly became my "Bull in the Ring," which had been the most hated and loved drill of my high school football career. When Coach sensed we were not really focused, or when we failed to execute plays properly, he would call for Bull in the Ring. The entire team would circle up and Coach would call out a number. The player with that number would move to the center of the ring. Coach would then call out a second number and that player would charge, full speed, toward the player in the ring. Mind you, the second player could be coming from anywhere in the circle— front, side, or behind the player in the center. As soon as Coach called the second number the player in the center began, sometimes frantically, to determine the direction from which the charging player was coming. To be hit from the side or back, especially by one of the bigger, faster players, was not an experience any of us relished.

There were days when I thought the Bull in the Ring of 1300 Joseph E. Boone Boulevard would be the death of me. As I stood in the center, I'd be charged in all directions. A leaking roof. Broken roll-up doors. Brick walls with new holes chiseled out by thieves, who would strike while the train rolled by, covering up the sounds of their hammers, and take off with thousands of dollars' worth of equipment. The building's heat and air systems didn't work, and ancient sewer and storm drain lines had to be removed and replaced. The electrical system was out of date and out of code compliance.

Valued at $1.6 million, the building donation was a huge blessing, but now that blessing was going to cost more than $10 million to renovate and turn into a place of usability and productivity. Of course, the ultimate goal was much more than usability. I wanted to create a space so clean, so well maintained, that anyone who entered it would feel an immediate sense of lift and possibility. This crusty, dilapidated warehouse needed to someday become a home that I myself would want to live and break bread in.

If I gave the challenges we faced too much thought, I ended up in the center of the ring and the task at hand charged me from every direction. Other days I put the building in the center and took a running start at it. We cleaned out years of leftover supplies and trash. We placed buckets and barrels under the worst roof leaks. We painted walls we knew we would eventually tear down just so we would have something new and fresh in the space. It was worth spending time to put the best, brightest face on what we had, because there was no way I was going to wait for "the perfect space" to start helping more people.

So it was that twenty-three years into my professional life, I was sleeping nights in a 210,000-square-foot warehouse in an incredibly dangerous neighborhood, acting as an amateur security guard in an effort to keep out thieves who had been breaking in nightly. I didn't know what I was doing; I was a tiny army without strategy or tactics. The hope was that my presence itself would be a deterrent. At least I had good backup. Those nights I spent "on duty," I sidled up next to a convicted drug kingpin who had been recently released from seven years in prison. He had come to church after hearing about the Ghetto Rev, and after getting to know him, I asked him to help me out. He now slept next to me on a worn-out sofa, barely big enough to hold his giant body, which was inked neck to toe with gang tattoos. On the other side of me a rough-and-tumble former motorcycle gang member slept upright, but soundly, in an old office chair. He was a longtime volunteer who had never been homeless—though people often assumed he was, thanks to his rough exterior, long knitted beard, and ponytail.

Strategically located an equal distance from each of the three of us was a large cardboard box with an array of firearms lying on top of it. Each was fully loaded with one in the chamber and the safety mechanism in the off position. Giant rats occupied the building and I actually felt concerned that a rat might climb on the box and cause one of the guns to discharge. The potential headline filled my thoughts: Man Shot and Killed by Rat while Sleeping between Two Burly Men. After just a few nights of this scenario, I moved to the rat-free environment of my truck, trying to stay awake all night after working all day.

About the rats. The first one I saw in the warehouse was the size of a full-grown, pond-nourished beaver that had spent most of its time lying on a riverbank eating and getting fat. Huge rats, I'm talking HUGE rats, had taken up residence in the building. If this was ever to be a home for families, we had to figure out how to exterminate hundreds of rodents large enough to carry away small children.

Because I'd like to avoid being arrested (again), I won't describe the various ways we rid the space of the long-tailed squatters. Suffice it to say that high-powered weapons, fierce felines, enough poison to fill an apothecary's cabinet, and perhaps even Molotov cocktails and flamethrowers may or may not have been options. We carried out dead rats in bags, buckets, on shovels, and in wheelbarrows. Legend has it that occasionally a staff member would open a pretty gift box on her desk only to discover the grandfather of all rats in the box looking up with a bone-chilling death stare.

For every rat we killed, it seemed that three more moved in. We realized pretty early in the game that killing rats was not going to solve our rodent issue. We would have to seal the building, replace broken block walls, repair openings in the roof, and do everything possible to prevent the rats from getting in. Very little money was spent to exterminate rats but thousands and thousands of dollars were spent to keep rats out.

FINDING A NEW SPACE was a huge step, but to really make use of it, we'd need to vastly expand our operating budget. We were still the nonprofit equivalent of a ma-and-pop shop, just barely keeping the lights on. We needed funding and we needed partners.

I met with dozens of people, and dozens of people told me pretty quickly they thought my entire vision for City of Refuge was crazy. Attempting to have a one-stop shop for those in crisis was a foolish undertaking. "Focus on doing one thing really well," they said. "Spreading yourself too thin will not allow for success," they said. "You're trying to do too much," they said. Volunteers offered their suggestions and insights, even though they showed up once every six to twelve months. Donors let me know that the reason they were not going to grant our request for funding was because we were trying to be "all things to all people." I was told I was foolish, unintelligent, stupid, misguided, arrogant, and doomed to failure.

I just kept going. Now that I was in nonprofit, benevolent-care work, holding back was not an option. The friends I was now meeting needed *everything,* and who was I to say that I would help them with *something,* but someone else would have to help them with the rest. No, a one-stop shop made sense, and if it made sense, then we would figure out how to not only build but maintain it and, eventually, expand it to offer the things that I didn't yet know we needed.

CHAPTER 6

A New Home

Family means nobody gets left behind—or forgotten.

— LILO, *from Lilo & Stitch**

If getting people to understand and support my practical vision of the One-Stop Shop was difficult, trying to explain the emotional vision was almost impossible.

I wanted to give people access to an environment like the one I had known all my life—safe, loving, and rich with opportunity, where good decisions could reliably lead to positive outcomes. I had read Dr. Martin Luther King Jr.'s vision of a "beloved community,"† where prejudice and racism didn't exist or determine who got what. This would be a community where reality as people had come to know it operated with completely different rules. "Fair" would actually mean something, and there would be no lost causes.

---

* *Lilo & Stitch,* written and directed by Chris Sanders and Dean DeBlois (2002, Los Angeles, Walt Disney Pictures).

† Martin Luther King Jr., http://www.thekingcenter.org/king-philosophy.

What that meant, to me personally, was that for anyone who needed it, we would become family. We would treat the whole person with the same patience and care as a family member. When our residents used our services, from health care to child care to counseling to job training, they would experience the same consideration, trust, and support you would expect to find in a loving home.

Love is a word that scares a lot of people. Very few people use the word outside of their immediate, biological families, but we do it a lot. (Three of our girls are now married. City of Refuge is the only upbringing they've known, so they were surprised to see that their husbands' first reactions to life on campus was some degree of culture shock. The men had to adapt to the unusual breadth and diversity of their new in-laws, as would most.)

We've found that familial love arises naturally when you're committed, daily, to finding and believing in the best of people. But we've also come to realize how deeply many of our residents need to hear the word itself. Some of them never have. Sometimes it takes years before we hear it back. Sometimes we never do. But I believe that each time they hear it, they get a step closer to trusting the good we see in them.

Vanessa Cowan is someone who told us from the get-go that she desperately needed a loving home. She's a good example of what I mean when I say we treat each person individually, like our own family.

Vanessa is just five years younger than I am. She was homeless when I met her. Not long after, she decided that I was going to take the place of the father she never knew. My family would be her family. I was honored, and also amused, because I'm not sure I ever had a choice. "Diddy" is what she called me. Rhonda became Mama and each of my daughters became "sister." (She could never remember which girl had which name—a common dilemma when you name your girls Kassi, Kelsi, Kensi, Kaylin, and Karli—so this was a practical choice.) We all settled into our roles and found ourselves answering to the names she had assigned us.

One summer, Vanessa was volunteering for us, and on a particularly humid day in mid-July she made her way down the length of the parking lot and ended up in my office. Due to poor health, basic everyday tasks of life, stuff most of us don't even think about, required an intense effort from Vanessa. She has a bad knee and diabetes, and is heavy enough that she can walk only a few feet without having to stop and rest. That day I heard her coming before I saw her, every breath labored, stopping often as she leaned against the wall to draw fresh oxygen into her lungs. She made her way uninvited into my office, sat down, and put both elbows on the desk as she sat and tried to calm her breathing enough to speak.

All I could do was push my chair back a bit and wait. Eventually, Vanessa spoke. "You got anything to drink in that refrigerator back there, Diddy?" she asked.

"Well, Vanessa," I answered, "I've got water bottles, lots of them."

Finally, I thought, I'll get Vanessa to drink some water. As her Diddy, I worried about her health. While eager to overcome decades of drug addiction, Vanessa had no interest in developing better nutritional habits. Her breakfast of choice was a family-sized bag of Cheetos and a two-liter Dr Pepper, and lunch or dinner weren't much better. She wanted her food fried and salted heavily. Suggestions that she drink water were met with scowls that burned holes in our souls.

Her response to my offer caught me by surprise and made me laugh out loud.

"Diddy," she huffed, "you better just give me a twenty and I'll get my own something to drink at the store across the street."

That she asked for a twenty in order to buy a two-dollar drink didn't surprise me at all. I knew three cans of dip and a bag of Cheetos or a package of cupcakes would accompany the soda. It was the fact that she was going to pad slowly back down the parking lot and work her way across four lanes of traffic and then walk half a block to the store just so she could have soda instead of water—that's what got me.

I opened my wallet and pulled out a twenty. I handed it to her and told her I loved her as she walked away with a big smile on her face.

Some might say I'm doing harm, feeding a tobacco and junk food addiction. But put yourself in Vanessa's body. She had walked away from heroin, crack cocaine, and alcoholism. Her knees hurt. Her back hurt. She was dragging her weight around a city that turned into a sweat lodge all summer long. Broccoli and water might bring some benefits, but sugar, bubbles, and tobacco, all packaged up nice? Guaranteed relief. Her walking to the store for a soda just wasn't something I was going to argue about, not that day anyway. Vanessa was family. There were days to push her about her diet and days to express my love and spot her a twenty.

You may have heard the saying that blood is thicker than water. There's another version: Blood is thicker than milk. The idea is that people who spill blood together, trusting each other on the field of battle, are bound even more closely than brothers raised on the same mother's milk. Sometimes I feel that way about our family. The struggles we've shared root us together as strongly as any family tree.

THE JOURNEY BETWEEN moving into the warehouse and opening our One Stop Shop to women like Vanessa was not an easy one. It took about two years and thousands upon thousands of man-and-woman-hours of hard work to make the warehouse even habitable. The rats were at bay, all systems functional, and the space bright with new lighting and fresh paint. We had even built basketball courts and started a nightly tradition of evening games for anyone who wanted some playtime after the strenuous focus of the day. The thieves were as busy as ever, but we thwarted what we could and saw the rest as the cost of doing business.

As we battled with the warehouse, we ramped up our regular offerings. To continue building relationships, we expanded our crisis programs. In addition to the street feedings twice a week, we now offered Safe Haven, where people could come for a hot meal, get a shower and haircut, and talk with social workers about their life challenges. We solicited food donations from grocery stores, churches, and businesses. We made great use of food left over from office parties, social functions, and family reunions. Add enough cheese or sauce to the right combination of leftovers, and suddenly you've got a tasty casserole. It turns out that really hungry people actually like and appreciate a good casserole. A little ingenuity went a long way in making healthy, appetizing food out of odds and ends.

We now had a big warehouse, but we were still a tiny, unproven organization that no one had really heard of, unless it was because I had directly solicited them to support the One Stop Shop, usually unsuccessfully. We had the vision, but we didn't yet have the trust or awareness among the kind of people who could give us the money to make it happen. We were

scrounging for resources, perpetually understaffed, and dealing with most of our days as an organization in reactive, not
proactive, mode. In short, we were like any start-up, short on
funding but long on passion. In 2005, the equation changed
dramatically.

That September, Hurricane Katrina devastated the coasts
of Louisiana and Mississippi and thousands were left without
homes. Though Atlanta is hundreds of miles away, we are the
region's urban hub. Calls began to come in from government
and social services agencies, inquiring about our ability to
provide temporary housing, serve as a distribution center for
personal and household items, and provide space to social
workers and staffers from various nonprofits who would
gather to offer services and resources to those fleeing the area
affected by the hurricane. Of course we agreed to serve in any
way possible.

Within a few days we had acquired bedding, opened up
space for folks to sleep, received truckloads of donations, and
established a Resource Center to serve individuals in crisis.
We were blessed to serve more than thirty-five hundred people with shelter, clothing, food, personal items, and options
for permanent relocation to the Atlanta area. We assisted
hundreds of families with furniture and other donated items,
with dozens of team members sorting those items and placing them in groupings that would go to homes depending on
family size. Hundreds of volunteers from the Metro Atlanta

area showed up, and we were interviewed on the radio and on television and written about in the newspapers. Suddenly we were viewed not just as a place that fed and clothed homeless people and offered an after-school program to kids, but also as a place that could rally volunteers, connect with resources, and generate financial donations. The hurricane relief effort was by far the largest undertaking we had been part of in our short time as an organization, and we pulled it off. We had an impact on thousands of individuals and families in positive ways, and the feeling among our staff that we could be agents of change on a bigger, more ambitious scale really took root. As we began to believe, other groups began to believe in us as well. Maybe I wasn't some nut sketching on napkins after all.

One such group was the Regional Commission on Homelessness in Atlanta. Under the leadership of Mayor Shirley Franklin, funds had been raised to address the homeless crisis in the city. Following the months of hurricane-relief housing, we had begun setting up beds nightly and having thirty to fifty homeless women from Atlanta sleep on campus. They had access to showers, meals, mail delivery, and other essentials. Debi Starnes from the mayor's office, a higher-level leader than I had even dreamed of reaching out to, called and asked for a meeting. In that meeting, the city proposed a grant to City of Refuge to renovate forty thousand square feet of our space into a transitional living center for single home-less women and their children. The city would provide the funds for renovation and City of Refuge would bear the re-sponsibility for the bulk of operating expenses moving for-ward, for a period of at least fifteen years. We agreed, and the city awarded $1.5 million for construction and furnishings of forty family units in the space.

Meanwhile, we were putting the finishing touches on our campus's new dining room: a giant, gleaming hall where we could serve five hundred guests at a time, alongside a fully equipped commercial kitchen. We raised additional dollars to build a child-care center so the children living on campus would have safe and quality care each day while the mothers were involved in working their individual case plans. We hired case managers and residential service associates, in-creased the number of kitchen staff, and prepared the space to welcome homeless mothers whom we believed, provided with the necessary resources, would move from struggle to self-sustainability.

If the first years of building City of Refuge were all about building trust, the next stage of our growth was all about re-ceiving. It continues to amaze me that our willingness to trust people we did not know to sleep in our space, spend time with our kids, and share our resources resulted in others trusting us to take *their* resources to serve even more individuals in need. Paying it forward takes on many shapes and forms, but the cycle of trust always has to start somewhere.

In 2008, forty mothers and eighty-two children moved in over the course of the first two weeks, and the space now known as Eden Village was suddenly alive, active, and full of possibility and potential. Partnerships with financial-literacy agencies, addiction recovery organizations, and mental health-care providers were established, and the news of our one-stop shop quickly spread. City of Refuge was not a shelter; rather, it was a transitional housing program that offered a continuum of care and a map to independence, with guides along the way to assist as needed. When people arrived, we'd talk them through the list of services. Watching their eyes go from dim with hopelessness to bright with optimism floored me every time. Occupancy was perpetually at 100 percent, with a waiting list.

Less than a year after opening the doors of Eden Village, the city called and asked if we could construct an additional housing facility inside the warehouse, this time for homeless single women without children. There was a deadline associated with the funding for the project, and in nothing short of a miracle we were able to get approval for the project, have a building permit in hand, complete construction, and welcome women into the space in less than three months. On the first day all eighty beds were occupied and capacity population has been the norm in both Eden Village I and Eden Village II for the past thirteen years. (Our property can physically accommodate only about five hundred housing requests a year. In 2017, we had more than seven thousand.) Hundreds of families have entered our doors and exited six months later. Moms graduate with the basic building blocks in place to create stable, secure lives for themselves and their children.

As in our earliest days, not every story was a success story. Some residents settled into our care like a soft cradle; they were very respectful and willing to trust in the framework we had established. They worked as hard as possible to achieve a better life. Others were manipulative, always trying to play an angle and take advantage of the system. Still others expressed anger that had pent up over many years of struggle and now seemed to erupt like a volcano spewing hot lava that threatened to consume anyone in its path. Like most places where large numbers of people live together, we had the ones whose stories made us weep but who nevertheless kept us laughing at the same time because of unique personalities that had survived the days of struggle.

VANESSA, whom you just met, first came to us not long after Eden Village opened its doors. I met her at a Sunday morning breakfast. She looked across the table at me and asked, "Can I go home with you?" That's not a question you get asked every day. Here was a homeless lady with an odor you could detect from far away and a dip of snuff the size of a lump of coal lodged between her cheek and gum. She wasn't asking to go to Eden Village, but to go to my home.

Still, I considered it. At that point, we didn't yet live on campus. We had thought we'd pack up from Fourteenth Street and move right in, but we soon learned that zoning prohibited it. Disappointed, we had purchased a home near our girls' school. Every bedroom was occupied and there was not a guest room.

But here I had a lady asking for help. She wanted to leave the streets and get away from the drugs. She wanted to escape the constant noise and potential violence, so she had asked if she could go home with me. Maybe more than most people, Vanessa knew exactly what she needed—and she was exactly the kind of individual for whom the One Stop Shop could make all the difference.

But Eden Village already had a waiting list a mile long. I stumbled for a bit to come up with an answer, and then it struck me. We had a home we had recently rented near the warehouse, where a woman named Ms. Sadie was running a drug rehabilitation program.

While not technically true, I told her that, yes, she could go home with me. After we completed meal service and cleanup, I walked Vanessa to my car and watched as she worked herself into the front seat. Managing her girth into the front seat of the Toyota Camry I was driving that morning nearly did her in. Sweat was running in rivers down her brow and face as I drove her to the house we called Shechem.

Shechem was one of the original Cities of Refuge in the Old Testament. The name means "strong shoulder." Shechem was run like a loving family home. It was stylishly decorated and scrupulously clean. All the residents helped maintain it, shared meals, and were encouraged to support one another with loving care.

Vanessa offered no resistance when I explained that she was not going to our personal home but to Shechem instead. She was weary beyond words, and I think just the thought of a hot shower and warm bed was more than she had dared to believe was possible when she awoke that morning after a night sleeping on concrete without so much as a blanket or pillow for comfort.

The story Vanessa told was foreign to me at the time, but unfortunately it is very similar to hundreds of stories I have heard since. My brother Jeff once interviewed her for the StoryCorps project, which seeks to preserve the American experience, much of which looks nothing like Norman Rockwell paintings.

"I didn't have no childhood," she told Jeff. She means it. Vanessa was twelve when her mother allowed a man from their neighborhood to sexually assault her in exchange for a fifth of liquor. "She did it because she loved the liquor. She was controlled by it. She didn't care 'bout nothin' else," said Vanessa, the tears running down her cheeks. Jeff and the facilitator were so upset and emotionally overwhelmed by her story that they couldn't speak, but Vanessa bravely moved the conversation forward.

Sex with her molester became a long-standing arrangement. At twelve years old, Vanessa became pregnant. Upon the birth of the child, the Department of Family and Children's Services took both Vanessa and the baby into custody. That was more than thirty-five years ago, and Vanessa never saw her child again. After spending the next seven years in foster care, Vanessa aged out of the system. With no family support she ended up on the streets, where she would live on and off for the next twenty-plus years. Heroin, crack cocaine, and her favorite, Colt 45 malt liquor, would be her companions nearly every day, at least every day she could figure out a way to get enough money to make a purchase. Stealing was her most common tool for getting what she needed, and prior to her sickness and incredible weight gain, prostitution helped fund her addictions. She had a second child, a son, who was being raised by his father's family, who prohibited her from seeing him.

We know that the financially poorest among us statistically have the poorest health. Of course, limited access to decent health care is part of that. But in Vanessa, as with so many others we meet, you could see that there was more at work. Barely forty, her body was breaking down, the effects of a life where she felt no control or security. Researchers tell us such a life chronically stresses every system of the body. Stress leads to inflammation, inflammation to disease. You might have heard this called *weathering*. Vanessa had lived a life of trauma all her conscious memory, and now, fulfilling the most basic tasks of taking care of herself was a struggle.

Again, put yourself in her body. Imagine you wake up one day, with back pain worse than usual, or maybe an infection that refuses to heal. You don't have a car. So if you want to see a doctor, you're going to have to find yourself bus fare, walk to the bus stop, get yourself on that bus, then endure a couple of miles of bumpy riding to Grady, the hospital in Atlanta that offers free services. You'll have to check yourself in. You may have to ask for help to fill out the forms, because you can't read or write, filling you with shame. You'll then sit on an uncomfortable bench built for someone, a Lilliputian maybe, but not for you, for hours. You're lucky if you get a doctor who takes your pain seriously and gives you a thorough exam. If he gives you meds, you've then got to get yourself to a pharmacy. . . . Have you given up yet? Me too. Here, have some dip and an adult beverage.

Although jail was not really a desirable option, Vanessa knew Fulton County guaranteed a bed and three meals a day, so she began to intentionally break the law as the number of years on the street began to add up. As time went on, Vanessa unfolded more details of her story, and I was struck by how desperate she had to have been the morning she asked if she could go home with me. She only knew me from the feeding line, and we had never had a real conversation. I doubt if she even knew my name. And yet, in a moment of combined hope and desperation, Vanessa asked for exactly what she needed—a new home.

CHAPTER 7

No Lost Causes

He that holds the handle of a frying pan
runs the risk of burning himself.

—FRENCH PROVERB

As Eden Village grew, City of Refuge was starting to feel less like a vision and more like our day-to-day. We had built a six-month program that offered a full array of support services to 225 women and children at a time. We had constructed a clinic that provided medical, dental, vision, and mental-health care. Our day care offered loving support to children aged six weeks to five years of age. A private school serving middle and high school students was having great success. Culinary arts training classes were well underway, the first of our programs to provide vocational training in high-demand occupations to anyone with an obstacle to employment. That included citizens returning from prison, veterans, those recovering from addiction, those coming out of homelessness, and those who did not complete high school.

Career development, job networking, and assistance with open legal, domestic violence, and DFCS cases were all available. We had built quality programs and now had the process and people to maintain them.

No longer in chaotic start-up mode, we had a somewhat orderly, relatively smoothly running operation. It was understandable, then, when some on my staff looked askance when I told them I was opening our doors to house a former gangbanger with a bond on his head, a PCP addiction, and a violent temper who was only two days removed from his life of crime.

Along this twenty-year journey I have made decisions that absolutely not one person on my staff agreed with, and while only a couple of them spoke up in this particular situation, I was well aware that even my most loyal inner circle were questioning my judgment. We had built so much, and people correctly perceived that the stakes were higher now. We had more people invested and more people depending on us. But I was clear. A larger organization meant nothing if it required us to dilute our commitment to welcoming even "lost causes." And so to top it off, I provided Ryan, the former gang member, with a master key to our facility.

Was I aware that the trust in that gesture could blow up not just in my face but in the face of our organization? You bet I was. I felt some anxiety, but I did it anyway because I believed Ryan desperately needed someone to believe in him.

He had lived most of his life at the uncanny junction between power and helplessness. If we wanted to help this grown man transform, we could not treat him like a child or, worse, like a criminal.

And yet if anyone needed the safe and complete enclosure of our eight-foot gates, it was Ryan Marchman. He was the kind of tough you get when you've never been able to trust that anybody, anywhere, truly had your back. Ryan had spent seventeen years of his life living off the bounty of others. When he was thirteen he was beaten by local gang members in his hometown, Cleveland, until he submitted to their demand that he join their gang. The experience scarred him in such a way that he developed a lifestyle of abusing others in order to numb his own wounds. As a teen and young adult, Ryan led crews that terrorized and robbed people, taking their belongings and often leaving them with both physical and emotional scars.

His biological father left before Ryan was old enough to develop a strong relationship with him. He grew up with his mother and his stepfather, Big Ivan, who had once been in the military and now was a heroin addict and alcoholic. As early as Ryan can remember, his stepfather would lock him in the dark basement of his home for hours at a time, guarded by a terrifying Haitian devil statue, while Ivan went on violent rampages upstairs. Terrified, Ryan hid under bags of clothing stored in the basement and prayed to a God he wasn't sure existed that he would be delivered from his prison of fear. When Ivan would finally leave the house, he'd hear his mother unlock the door, and he'd race up the stairs into her arms. Often she'd have a black eye or a bloody lip. "It'll get better," she'd tell him.

Finally, when he was thirteen, he watched Ivan torture his mother by dumping water on her head and beating her with the bucket. Ryan lost it and screamed at Ivan to leave her alone. He was still a little guy and didn't have a chance when Ivan charged him. Ryan remembers, "He destroyed me. He picked me up, dragged me around the house. He punched me, he gave me a concussion, he broke my collarbone. Gave me fractured ribs, and I was hospitalized."

When Ryan finally got home, his mother sat him down and offered a prelude to bad news: "God teaches that people deserve forgiveness." Ivan was moving back in. Ryan was furious and terrified, and he ran away that night. He wandered from place to place, first staying with local prostitutes, who handed him off to a house where a bunch of gang members were living. "We got your back, man," they said.

"I was looking for protection," says Ryan. "I was scared. I was looking for a family, and they became that family." My stomach lurched when he described his initiation. It was an ultraviolent version of the same drill I knew as Bull in the Ring, except Ryan was a thirteen-year-old beaten mercilessly by grown men. He tried to run away and they chased him down. "It's too late. You're already in. If you leave, we'll kill you," they said. "And by the way, you've got to start putting in work." His first job was to fire shots at a gathering of rival gang members. The driver on this hit helped him ease his panic with his first dose of PCP.

Over time, he sank deeply into his addictions, his uncontrollable temper, and a heavy feeling of hopelessness. Years of armed robberies, hits, drug sales, arson, and a long stint in juvie earned him status in the gang. By thirty, Ryan was powerful, and reckless. He added cocaine to his PCP habit, and he put together a crew whose "whole mission" was robbing rival dealers. "We thought we were invincible. We stopped wearing masks," he says. Unsurprisingly, they became unpopular. The executions began. Soon his crew of twenty was down to three men. One day in a gas station, a hit man surprised him. Ryan stood feet from a gun aimed at his face. His assailant pulled the trigger. The gun jammed and the guy took off. So did Ryan, to Atlanta, where his mother lived, just a few blocks from City of Refuge.

He didn't wait long to start building a new crew in Atlanta. The few friendly contacts he had left back in Cleveland ran drugs in for him, and he gained territory quickly. Months turned into years, during which time he got married—in retrospect, a mistake, one that might have ended quickly and uneventfully, except that one day he came home and found her in bed with another man. He flew into a blind fury and a loud and violent argument with the man ended with Ryan throwing him out a window. Then Ryan held a gun to his wife's head—and was interrupted by police.

Ryan spent a year in prison waiting for his hearing. When it finally arrived, he was facing twenty years and was completely numb and defeated. He didn't bother to hire a lawyer, but at his hearing, his family pleaded on his behalf. He was released on bond.

"I went straight back out on the corner," he says. Not long after, high on cocaine, he came up with a plan to rob a kingpin named Smooth and use the proceeds to relocate to a new city, leaving his legal mess behind.

RYAN'S STORY MIGHT have continued its violent path from here to eternity—except it didn't. Something strange happened the day of the planned robbery. Ryan and his crew crept onto the property, guns drawn. Ryan's heart was beating out of his chest. This should have been just another job. But high on cocaine and adrenaline, he began to tremble. It was as though years of repressed pain, terror, and exhaustion had suddenly caught up with him. As the men prepared to move, he backed away.

"What you doing man? You trippin', you trippin'!," he remembers his gunmen saying. "I was like, 'I can't. I can't. I don't know what's wrong with me.'"

At first he thought it was the cocaine. But as he walked home, Ryan began to weep. "I had no idea what was happening to me," Ryan says. "I was shaking and crying. I was a mess and I hadn't cried since my stepdad broke my collarbone. Now, for no reason, I could not stop crying."

When he got home, his mother was on the porch talking to her next-door neighbor, Greg Washington, who was a volunteer at City of Refuge. Any other day, Ryan would have been furious to see Greg. He had heard about this next-door neighbor who disapproved of the gang gatherings that were now happening outside his home on a daily basis. In fact, he had Greg on his mental hit list.

But at this moment, Greg was living, breathing hope. He told Ryan his story. In the late '80s and early '90s, he had distributed cocaine up and down the Eastern Seaboard, until he was busted and sentenced to twenty years. He spent several years in the federal penitentiary and had been paroled just months before, released into his mother's care, in the house next door to Ryan's family. He told Ryan about me and City of Refuge, where he was also a member of our church.

Ryan was moved by the passion and energy Greg exuded as he spoke of the ministry, as well as the look of peace and contentment on Greg's face. He asked Greg if he could meet the people who ran City of Refuge. Greg brought Ryan to the warehouse and connected him with one of the senior leadership team members, who was leading a Bible study that Ryan joined—and found it to be a circle of support and humility like nothing he had ever experienced. After long conversations and much soul-searching, Ryan decided: "Man, I'm ready to give that life up." Since City of Refuge is an organization birthed out of a deep faith experience, one of the staff pastors prayed with Ryan and a plan was set in motion to begin the process of redirecting every aspect of his life.

Ryan told Greg right away that he couldn't go back home. His gang here had the same rules he knew from Cleveland: Once you're in, you're in for life. There would be serious consequences to pay. There was no way he could live with his mother. His brother, who remained in the gang, lived there still.

At this point, Greg introduced me to Ryan. We sat down together, and he told me his story much as I've recounted it here. Immediately I knew we would circle him into our arms, whatever it took.

There was the small problem that all our formal housing programs within the warehouse were for women. However, the main building had one section that had been built out and used as offices. There were many small empty rooms in that space. I invited Ryan to move into one of them. There was only room for a twin bed, a dresser, and a chair. Even a monk might have requested a few more square feet. The bathroom was down the hall and a shower room was even farther away. Without hesitation, Ryan accepted the offer and moved in.

For months, Ryan did exceptionally well with only brief moments of rebellion, anger, or depression. He'd get lonely and fearful that his former gang members would come after him. Now that he was making only ten dollars an hour working for us, not having money was another source of frustration. Unsurprisingly, it wasn't so easy to exchange the only lifestyle he knew for tough emotional labor carried out in a converted warehouse with a leaky ceiling and, yes, some rats still. Sometime after settling into the routine of his new life, he began to hear the street calling to him again.

We almost lost Ryan more than once. In just one episode that leaps to memory, I arrived at work one morning and was informed that Ryan had left during the night and had not returned to campus. I began to call his cell phone with no luck. The girl he was dating did not know where he was. A bit of anxiousness rose up in me. I was well aware, along with everyone else, that Ryan had the key to all the doors on campus and had access to the keys to City of Refuge vehicles. Surely Ryan himself wouldn't steal from us or bring violence to campus . . . or would he? If he was high and in a state of emotional crisis, whose hands might those keys end up in? Worrying was pointless. All I could do was bring him back before the question was answered.

Jeff began canvassing the neighborhood, knocking on doors for information, and we soon knew where Ryan was. Our fears were confirmed—he was back with his gang and they had been out all night on a robbing spree. Ryan and other gang members were gathered on a street well-known for drugs, guns, and gangs. A friend was on campus that day doing some consulting work, and knowing that the gang members would recognize my vehicle, I asked to borrow the keys to his BMW 750, which he reluctantly handed over. Steve Grimes got into the front passenger seat and Jeff jumped in the back. I headed rapidly to the street where we had been told Ryan was.

I pulled into the driveway of the address we'd been given and exited the car without thinking. I walked around the house to the backyard, oblivious to what might be there. Several guys were in the yard and there were tables set up with guns and drugs sorted and stacked on the tables. My sudden appearance startled the group and a couple sprinted around to the other side of the house. Two more ran into the house, leaving three who stood looking at me as though I were from another galaxy. Making sure I scored first, I screamed, "Where's Ryan?! Tell me right now where he is!"

"We don't know Ryan. What you talking about, man?" one of the guys responded.

"I know he was here. Now tell me where to find him!" I yelled a bit more loudly. I could see that the guys thought I was alone and not carrying a gun, and I braced myself for an angry retaliation. Technically, since Steve and Jeff had remained in the safe confines of the car, I *was* alone, and I didn't have a gun, but I was not about to back down now. Sometimes you are so far in the tunnel you may as well continue to see what's on the other side of the darkness.

Suddenly I heard Jeff calling my name and saying, "Bruce, Ryan's out here, he's out here!" Running back around the house I saw Ryan, hoodie pulled over his head, jump into a vehicle and take off like a rabbit trying to escape the snake that intends to have it for dinner. I backed my friend's BMW out of the driveway and took off after him. I'm sure I more than doubled the speed limit on those residential streets, weaving and turning left and right and left again. Ryan was determined to get away and I was determined not to let him.

Turning left again, I realized that we were now on a dead-end street with a cul-de-sac turnaround at the bottom of a slight hill. As Ryan made the turn to come back up the hill, I slid the BMW across the street, blocking his only way of escape. Ryan slid to a stop just inches from the driver's-side door of our car, and we were literally just a few feet from each other. I clenched the steering wheel, heart pumping, breath ragged, mind spinning, and stared at Ryan, who had his head down and his hands out of sight.

Slowly he lifted his head and pulled back the hood of the sweatshirt he was wearing. Panic grabbed me by the throat as I realized the man looking at me was not Ryan. They had sent a decoy out to lead us away while Ryan relocated. Anger overtook the panic, and I determined to simply sit there, blocking his way. The driver and I glared at each other for a few moments and then he lifted his right hand and laid a gun on the dashboard of the car, making sure the barrel of the gun was pointed in my direction.

I heard Jeff speak from the back seat. "Bruce," he said. "What?" I uttered with frustration. "He's got a gun and we don't," he stated calmly but matter-of-factly. Wisdom sometimes comes from the back seat of a borrowed BMW, so I put the car into reverse and backed out of the criminal's way. He removed the gun from the dash and, smirking, drove away without looking back. We returned in silence to the warehouse, and as I handed my friend his keys, I said, "Don't turn left when you leave campus today."

Ryan called a couple days later and asked if he could see me. At that point, I was angry and second-guessing myself. Maybe I had finally taken on a case whose sad history had left him unredeemable. Maybe I was putting myself and others in too much danger for a father and husband to justify. But finally, I pushed all those feelings aside and said yes. I owed him at least a meeting.

Looking as though he had been dragged for miles by a team of horses, he slumped into a chair across from me and laid the keys to our property on the desk. Head bowed, he came clean. "I was out there robbing people. Doing stupid stuff," he said. He didn't expect to be forgiven, but said that he was sorry, and sorry for putting us at risk. True regret filled his voice, and while I was still angry with him, I reminded myself that trusting someone means nothing if you immediately recant when they mess up—especially someone with a history as traumatic as Ryan's. Also, I was the one who had chosen to drive to gang headquarters and get into a car chase. After taking ownership, I began to feel genuine compassion again for this man who had been beaten and abused most of his life, by both his real family and his adopted one. Just because we had given him a place to sleep and a job did not mean we had rebuilt what had been broken.

I pushed the keys back in Ryan's direction. He looked at me, not understanding. "Are you ready to do this?" His eyes flashed with surprise, and he nodded.

"Then let's start over."

I told him to get a shower, get some rest, and be ready to go back to work the next day. His tears told me I had made the right decision, even though many would rightfully question it. He told me later he couldn't believe I wasn't throwing him away. This second chance, offered by a man he admired, who had become a father figure, flooded his body like an antidote to a poison.

Ryan was thirty when he arrived, but it was with us that he went through many of life's positive rites of passage. He played in our weekly basketball game. He had his first birthday party with cake and candles and singing. He received his first presents under the Christmas tree. On his first Easter, long after my girls had left the table, Ryan was still there, concentrated as a bomb tech on the project of dipping eggs in coffee mugs of brightly colored dye. When he started his first job, working in the warehouse for Compassion Atlanta with Steve, he told us he had been driving illegally his entire life. So we took him to take his driving test and get his first license. He earned his GED. He opened his first bank account and learned to budget. He learned to pray.

When he had arrived on campus, he was still wanted by the state of Georgia. Steve set up a meeting, and the police took Ryan to jail briefly before a court hearing. We advocated for him, convincing the judge to sentence him to probation under the First Offender's act. He was released to our care with requirements that he complete anger management and counseling.

Over time, there were moments where we could all see and feel tectonic change happening—like the first time he got to speak on the phone with his daughter. The last time he had seen her was back in Cleveland, when she was three or four years old. He was known for dressing her in gang colors and hanging out on the corner with her. Then one day, he had buckled her into the back seat of his car, something he had done many times before. No car seat, just the belt. As Ryan drove the streets of the hood, a rival gang member spotted him and fired shots at the car. "I remember speeding off, and then looking back, like scared, trying to feel for her," said Ryan. "She was screaming, so I didn't know if she was shot or not." He sped to the home of the child's mother in a panic. His daughter was fine, but unsurprisingly, her mother was not. "You'll never get her again," she said. And thankfully for all involved, she meant it. They moved and kept the location from Ryan, completely disappearing from his life.

A few years after his arrival at City of Refuge, Ryan got a phone message. It was his daughter's mother. She had found his Facebook account. Ryan's feed showed photo after photo of his volunteering with us—out with Greg Washington in the community, feeding people, smiling with other volunteers. What a contrast with the man she knew from the corner. "I'll let you talk to her now, if you start paying child support," she told him. He started sending checks, and soon he was having regular conversations with his teenage daughter.

Ryan was healing old wounds and building his life with us, but his day-to-day was still a roller coaster. The new relationship with his daughter was welcome but emotionally heavy. He'd get depressed and angry and lash out. A lot was on his shoulders. I stayed focused on the present, prepared to help with every emotional and practical hurdle. And there were many. But each precious day he woke up sober, focused on small steps forward, justified all the work of the days before.

Was I still scared of what the future might bring? Yes.

But as with so many people who would drive past the guard booth into our campus, I trusted that change would happen if we kept him close, listened to his pain, endured his anger, and held him as tightly as the lioness holds her cubs when the predator approaches.

CHAPTER 8

The Old Red Truck

I can't believe the news today /
Oh, I can't close my eyes and make it go away.

—BONO *and* THE EDGE,
"SUNDAY BLOODY SUNDAY"

Funerals have caused me to shed more tears more than I am comfortable with, and honestly, have many times left me feeling angry. My faith stands strong but there have been days when I've felt it tumble. Funerals are often the cause.

As a pastor's son I attended far more than my share growing up. I was never consulted as to whether or not I wanted to go; I was just told to put on my nice clothes and get in the car. I've never liked funerals; as an adult, it has gotten much worse. Serving as a minister myself, I've officiated far more funerals than I wish to recall. I've penned words that I hoped would bring comfort. Of course, even harder are the funerals where I am among those receiving the condolences. I've known and loved too many folks who came to us because they struggled with life and then were rudely interrupted by death. Some left us at low points, others as they fought to recover. But so many leave this world early, violently, or alone.

Skipping funerals is bad protocol, but I'll admit that I do it. From making excuses to scheduling meetings during the time a funeral is taking place, I'm guilty. There have been funerals I wanted to skip but had to attend because I was the officiating minister. Such was the case with the service for a man named Harold. I'd known one of Harold's sons for several years—an ex-con with a history of violent behavior—but had never met Harold or anyone else present that day.

The family decided to bury Harold as he had lived, I was told, so they had him dressed in blue jeans and a flannel shirt with a pack of Marlboro cigarettes and a lottery ticket stuck in the shirt pocket. That, in and of itself, caused me to look curiously into the coffin at Harold and wonder what he'd think of his final attire. Jeff was standing beside me at the coffin and I felt him lean in my direction, which could mean only one thing—he had something to say that he wanted only me to hear. I tilted my head in his direction and he spoke words that live in infamy: "You think we ought to check that lottery ticket?" We never checked, but Jeff's joking brought me up enough to make my remarks. Sometimes humor is the only thing that can get me through another sad ceremony. Harold, at least, died old, surrounded by family.

SINCE WE MOVED into the warehouse, my friend Jake had been working with Steve on our Compassion Atlanta project, which collected and distributed food and other resources around the city. Jake ran the floor, checking in inventory, sending it out, and keeping the space clean and organized. He also put his landscaping skills to use, cleaning up the back of the property. He had a vision for the space that included terracing the hill and installing a koi pond and a fountain. He'd tell you about it during the many hours he spent polishing his golf clubs.

Despite these dreams, Jake was as volatile as he'd ever been. We'd have a few great weeks, followed by another derailment that led him back into the abyss of addiction or mental illness. We'd lose track of Jake and discover later that he had been in the hospital or jail or had found a ride to Macon to visit his daughter.

And yet I'd now known him for more than a decade. If I could trust anything, it was that Jake, too, came back. Whatever addictions or demons pulled him away, he was always drawn back to City of Refuge by the magnets of love and acceptance he knew were waiting for him on campus. Staying angry with Jake was an impossible task. He'd envelop us with his good nature, big smile, and clear gratitude for the help we provided. Any frustration dissipated and was quickly replaced by a spirit of geniality. It was just impossible not to enjoy his company.

Jake had been gone for an unusually long stretch of months when he walked onto campus one day and made his way to my office. I was glad to see him and said so, suppressing the urge to ask where he'd been for so long. Maybe later. He asked if he could shower, shave, and get a fresh change of clothes.

I soon learned that he was newly released from another stint in jail, this time on a disturbing the peace and resisting arrest charge. By the time he was processed through the incredibly slow legal system and finally stood before a judge, six months or more had passed. Otherwise put, a seventy-year-old man spent a good chunk of his year incarcerated for behavior that goes unchecked on fraternity row in many college towns. The judge sentenced him to time served, and he was free again.

Jake always said about prison, if you don't do your time, it'll do you. This time, it seemed to have done him. His mental health had deteriorated a good bit, and Jake was in the worst physical condition we had ever seen him. He had always struck me as being as solid as his golf clubs. Not now. He was beaten down and losing his grip.

After this last stint in jail, Jake spent several weeks doing not much more than sitting at the picnic table in the back of the property cleaning his golf clubs. Taking Jake to high-end courses to play a round of golf had always been a complicated experience. Once I got him on the first tee, he was good to go, but everything leading up to that point was a challenge. He didn't want the attendant carrying his twenty-year-old bag with metal shaft irons and persimmon wood clubs to the cart; he trusted no one and wanted to carry his own clubs. He didn't like riding in the golf cart; real men walked the course and carried their own bags. There were no mulligans or gimme putts with Jake; you played every ball where it lay, as it lay, and you putted until the ball hit the bottom of the cup. On most of the courses where I took Jake, he was one of a very few people of color, and he always seemed to be looking over his shoulder, watching his back, making sure everything was good.

Jake liked to share pointers with me along the way in an effort to improve my swing. I enjoy golf but I'm not what you would call a good golfer. He was determined to fix that. He would emphasize a strong grip, a fluid backswing, a powerful movement forward at the top, and a nearly violent hip turn as the club head struck the ball. I'd entertain Jake's suggestions for a bit and then revert back to my move of choice— short backswing, little hip movement, and a forward swing made up primarily of arms with very little lower body or shoulder help. Jake would shake his head, spit on the ground, and hit a screaming drive right down Broadway.

Now he was standing for hours just practicing his swing, which was still fluid and flawless. But Jake was now much like a little child, good one moment and acting out inappropriately the next. Someone might walk too close and see him fly into a rage. He was well aware of his condition, and rather than sleep in a guest room in the warehouse, Jake asked if I would mind if he slept in the back seat of a Ford F-150 king cab truck I had parked on campus while waiting for the auto shop to perform some repairs. As was usually the case when Jake asked for something, I said yes. He started spending some nights in the truck, his golf bag on the floor beside him. Other nights he just wouldn't show up—no word, no call, no explanation. My friend Jake seemed to be wandering again with no home and no hope.

I REMEMBER IT as clearly as though it was yesterday. It was a Monday morning when Steve Grimes walked into my office and said, "Someone's sleeping in your truck and I can't get them to wake up. It's not Jake, this is a much bigger guy. The truck is locked and I've knocked and knocked but he won't stir at all." Steve and I walked down the parking lot to the truck. I peered through the back window of the driver's side and my heart sank before hardening to shock. In that moment, I felt blank and empty. Looking at Steve, I said, "It's Jake, and he's dead."

Jake had most likely climbed into the back seat of the truck sometime during the night on either Friday or Saturday and died in his sleep. The weather was hot and his body was bloated. I noticed his golf bag lying on the floor of the truck and I fought back tears. Picking up my phone, I instinctively dialed 911, telling the operator that a deceased man was in a vehicle on our property. She asked for the address, approximate age of the individual, where exactly on the property the vehicle was parked, and other details. We both sounded so clinical.

Moments later a fire truck arrived, followed by an ambulance and two police cruisers. Finding the doors to the truck locked, a strong, young fireman used a large ax to shatter the window. It all seemed to be happening in slow motion, surreal but harsh and jarring. As the window shattered, the smell of death rushed from the truck and a wave of nausea swept over me. Grown men stepped away.

Kelsi, our second-oldest daughter, was leading a tour of visitors around campus and they began making their way down the parking lot toward our location. I caught her eye and waved her away. I knew how much Jake meant to Kelsi and her sisters, and seeing him like this would be more than she needed to experience.

The firemen left quickly; no work left for them to do. The paramedics took notes, gathered what little info we could provide, and packed up, headed to assist those still with breath in their being. The coroner's office staff arrived and removed the body from the truck, joking about the weight, the tight quarters, and the smell. Fighting back anger and working hard to not say what I wanted to say, I reminded myself that these guys did this every day and joking was a coping mechanism they employed to prevent them from becoming overwhelmed. I think back now to Harold's lottery ticket. But unlike me, these men didn't attempt to keep their jokes private because it never occurred to them that I might love Jake like a member of my family. Even now, I guess that makes me angry.

The men laid Jake down on the asphalt parking lot and began asking us questions regarding his family and address. I explained his circumstances. By this point, he wasn't seeing much of his daughter down in Macon. They started looking through his pockets to see if he had an address book or anything that might shed some light on ways to reach family members. Thankfully they found what they were looking for—a little book with names, numbers, addresses, and miscellaneous notes. Jake's daughter's name was there with her address and phone number. They would call her a bit later and share the news of her father's unfortunate death. Receiving news of this nature from a complete stranger has to be extremely troubling, but the coroner's office insisted on making the call and would not share her number with us.

Jake was loaded into the back of the coroner's vehicle and driven away by a couple of guys whose names I did not get. Just like that, my friend was gone. I called Rhonda and the girls and shared the news. I didn't want them to hear it from someone other than me. Tears flowed freely and a leaden sadness settled over us.

After spending time alone in my office trying to process what had taken place, I made my way back to the truck and opened the back door. The only thing there was Jake's golf bag. Carrying the golf bag back to my office, I noticed staff members giving me a clear path. They knew Jake meant a lot to my family and I believe they were at a loss as to what to say. They chose to give me space rather than risk saying the wrong thing.

The bag held some golf balls, tees, and his ancient set of irons. His woods were gone, which meant he had sold them or pawned them for a few dollars to buy a bag of crack. Jake's level of desperation in his last days had to have been extremely high if it led him to sacrifice his golf clubs, his most prized possession. No clothes, no bag, no personal items, just his golf bag and clubs, that's all Jake left behind. I'm not ashamed to say that anger and frustration consumed me. Jake had eaten with me, laughed with me, and worshipped with me for years. And still he had died alone and broken, in an old red truck.

————

MAYBE MORE THAN any of the folks whom I've had the privilege to know at City of Refuge, Jake had captured my heart. Maybe it was the way he loved my girls, or maybe it was the glint in his eye when he knew I had caught him in a lie. His honesty about life and his own shortcomings in that life were refreshing. Jake never blamed anyone for his plight. He owned his failures just as much as he did his flawless golf swing.

Growing up I often heard my dad say, especially in times of tragedy, pain, and death, that God has a plan, and even when we don't understand, we just have to trust. Those are good words and I live by them most of the time. However, in the days after I found Jake dead, those words and most other words meant little. The abiding trust that had become a rhythm of life as natural as my heartbeat seemed to be in cardiac arrest. We had invested years of time, resources, love, and affection in Jake and now he was gone. He never got to see the redemption, restoration, and freedom that he longed for when he was well. His last days were filled with physical pain, mental battles, moments of surrender to the void of addiction, and nights spent either on the streets or in the back seat of my truck.

In my grief, I dug up an old recorded sermon I had written about my friendship with Jake. As I drove home from the warehouse that night, I listened to the cassette tape and wept without restraint. That night I couldn't sleep. I found myself at 4:30 a.m. standing in the shower weeping again. Jake represented so many we had known, so much we had done. He became the face of the hundreds of people who had come to us in trust, with the promise of a better tomorrow, and found only fleeting success or none. They haunted me. There was L.C., whom we had abruptly lost contact with. I have no idea if he is alive or dead, free or incarcerated, sober or addicted. Gloria, who, after years of wandering the streets with her sister and children, had died a slow, painful death in a nursing home in her forties, a statistically normal death for a woman who is homeless. She spent most of her last days alone in a coma-like state. We were notified after the fact.

Jake's daughter connected with my staff and arrangements were made for his farewell service in Atlanta. A few family members and a group of guys who knew Jake before his descent into addiction planned a funeral and meal to follow. Jake would not leave the earth without fanfare. There would be songs, sermons, stories, and reflections. Friends would have some food and would reminisce about the good times and the tough times they had experienced with their friend, Jake.

I assume this is how the day unfolded, but I can't say for sure. While the funeral was taking place, I sat at my desk and worked. I didn't have a meeting to attend or an event I was obligated to speak at. My calendar was clear, but I just didn't go. I didn't want to see an open coffin with Jake lying in it. It was too sad for me to face. And I was angry—at everything. At Jake for his decline. At a society that never gave him a chance. At a system that would lock up an old guy with mental disorders. I had done everything I could for the man in life, but having to attend his funeral was more than I could bear. Jeff and Steve and a few other staff members attended and relayed to me that it was a sweet service filled with good people who had loved Jake like we loved Jake. When the folks in charge discovered that Jeff was from City of Refuge, they brought him to the stage and seated him there for the entirety of the service. They also insisted that he share some thoughts regarding Jake and our friendship with him, and Jeff was glad to do so.

All around me, City of Refuge was thriving and growing. Every day as I walked the campus, I was getting stopped by visitors—sometimes volunteers, sometimes former residents—thanking me for my vision. I was receiving awards and being called words like *rebel* and *pioneer*. Meanwhile, inside, I struggled with my life's lowest point. For months after, the weight of Jake's death pressed down on my chest. I found it hard to breathe at times, and I was often fatigued. I was still fulfilling all the responsibilities of life, work, and fatherhood but not easily or with my usual joy and focus. It seemed that no one could help lift this load. For perhaps the first time in life, I didn't know who or what or how to trust.

I had so many what-ifs. Was there more I could have done, a way I could have led Jake—carried him, even—to a better, more comfortable end? L. C. had told me I couldn't save everyone. I thought I had accepted that. But in the end if I couldn't even save my friend, what was the point? A thousand questions and no answers. I was walking the valley of the shadow of death and feeling no comfort.

No, I DIDN'T ATTEND Jake's funeral. I'm not sure I'd make a different choice today. Yet the simple xeroxed flyer his family made to announce the memorial, with an image of his dignified, weathered face, still sits on my desk. His golf clubs still rest in my office closet.

I had my times with Jake, hundreds of them. I heard Jake laugh and I heard him curse. I heard him offer his thanks for what we gladly provided, and I watched him slip out the back with a few things we didn't. I watched Jake balance my girls on his knees and patiently correct my golf swing.

Do I wish things had turned out differently? Of course I do. But finally I stopped thinking of Jake as someone who died alone and broken in a truck. He is someone who lived on his own terms and who decided to come home to die. The old crusty guy I'd seen across the street years before, the one who invited others to our dinner table, the one who gave me my nickname and knew without question that we loved him, that guy had come to the place where he knew he was accepted just as he was. I think Jake knew that I'd be okay if he died in my truck, and I know I preferred him to die there than under a bridge in the city.

Over time, as my grief ebbed, I stopped wondering if I had done enough. Of course I could have done more—I can always do more. But at what cost? I thought about Sam, a vet with alcoholism, PTSD, and bipolar disorder who had been living under a bridge for ten years. I had met him in our Under the Bridge outreach to vets, one of many efforts that had at times removed me from Jake's side. Sam had now been sober and back on his feet for fifteen years. If I had spent more time with Jake, could I have helped Sam—and would it really have made the difference for Jake, bar none the most stubborn, self-possessed man I have ever met?

In the front pocket of the worn, stained jeans Jake died in, one of the coroner's staff had discovered a small green New Testament. I recognized it as the one I had given him years earlier. Flipping through it, I found he had circled the red letters of John 3:16, the verse of scripture most often associated with the Christian faith. That scripture reads, "For God so loved the world, that He gave His only begotten Son so that whoever believes in Him will not perish but have everlasting life."

Many people have something they hold on to, something they value, something that gives them hope. John 3:16 is foundational to those of us who embrace the Christian faith. Seeing that Jake had circled those words gave me some level of peace that came from knowing that he, too, had embraced those words of hope.

When people question my sanity for holding people close even when they have fallen time and time again, I feel the urge to remind them that devotion to *anything* in this material world is a little bit unhinged. Why love, why fight, why nurture when our lives are so short, so seemingly insignificant? Nothing lasts.

Jake did the best he could just as I did the best I could. I celebrate the moments of joy and brotherhood we shared. If we withhold our love today because we fear despair tomorrow—no matter how inevitable it may be—we sacrifice everything.

Section Three

CHAPTER 9

Let It Shine

Transformed people transform people.

—RICHARD ROHR[*]

After years chewing on the question of what transformation means, and seeing thousands of people transformed, I've arrived at thousands of answers. But there's one that always satisfies me. Transformation is finding that place where you not only enjoy the dignity of taking care of yourself but also the dignity of taking care of others.

Today, a third of City of Refuge's staff used to live on our campus, went through one of our programs, or came to us following incarceration. Warriors for justice, they now give daily of their time, talent, and treasure in an effort to help others who are starting their own journey to health and wholeness. Their light shines out and improves the lives of many.

---

[*] Richard Rohr, "Mysticism in Religion: Three Ways to View the Sunset," *Huffington Post*, February 11, 2011, https://www.huffingtonpost.com/fr-richard-rohr/three-ways -to-view-the-su_b_822092.html.

By this definition of transformation, and so many others, Ryan takes a crown. During many rocky years, he never gave up and neither did we. He kept a crazy schedule, balancing probation requirements against anger management and counseling and work and volunteering. We started helping him look for employment outside of campus. It was an incredibly depressing experience. Nobody would hire him. Dozens of times he responded to ads or even went on interviews arranged by people connected to our organization. And every time, he was turned away. He remembers naively thinking, "I had thought because I became Christian, everything was going to change, but I still had a record." His charges were too violent to take the chance, employers told him.

Finally, as Eden Village grew, we were able to hire Ryan full time. He became our night-shift security guard and spent countless hours sitting in the booth and walking the grounds. He still struggled with black moods and a temper. I honestly didn't know what his future held, but there were times it was hard to imagine him ever living independently.

And yet Ryan had made some huge strides in healing the internal wounds that made him so volatile. I mentioned earlier that he had reconnected on the phone with his daughter. This was a major step. Still, the experience that he says really turned his life around came later. For weeks, he had been frustrated with a sermon I had given on forgiveness. I had said that not forgiving someone is like drinking poison and hoping the one who wronged you dies. You could say Ryan wasn't picking up what I had dropped. To him, *forgiveness* was what had left him unprotected from an abusive stepfather. *Forgiveness* had delivered him to gang life. How different might his future have been if his mother had turned Ivan away for good? When it came to the topic of forgiveness, Ryan kept coming to the same conclusion: "No, you don't forgive anybody." The whole idea seemed really stupid—and yet it created a little burning ember somewhere deep inside him. It refused to go out.

ONE DAY, sitting in the guard booth, that ember ignited. Ryan heard a voice in his head. "Call Big Ivan. Call Big Ivan," it said. Ryan will say God was speaking to him. Whether we see it as divine or not, I think we've all had the experience of a nagging voice in our head expressing a thought or idea that something in us knows is right, even though we're not ready to admit it, let alone act on it. The voice may nag for days, months, even years before we finally heed it.

At first, Ryan fought this thought he'd had about Ivan. "Even having been at City of Refuge for years, I stilled boiled with anger any time that name started going in my mind. Call him? No way, I hate this dude. But the name haunted me the whole day," he says.

Finally Ryan decided to call his half sister.

"This is going to sound crazy," he told her. "I need your dad's number."

"Why would you want to talk to my dad? That didn't end good," she answered.

"I don't know why, but it's something I need to do."

She paused for a second. Ryan waited.

"Actually, I'm here at the hospital with him. So I'll give him the phone."

There was another pause, enough time for Ryan to get incredibly nervous. When Ivan finally answered, his "hello" was raspy and thin.

"Hey, Big Ivan, this is Ryan," was all Ryan could say, before Ivan cut in.

"Let me just say something," said the man who had terrorized the boy. "I'm so sorry for what I did to you and your mother. I got clean from drugs. I've been clean for years." He briefly filled Ryan in on how he had spent the intervening years. Finally, he said the words that Ryan didn't understand, until that moment, that he needed to hear: "Man, would you please forgive me for what I did? There's no excuses for what I did, and I'm sorry."

Ryan accepted his apology. In a dreamlike state, he found himself apologizing, too, for not being the best stepson. Perhaps the words were an unconscious apology to himself for the life he had lived after.

He and Ivan agreed to talk again in the future. "I hung up

the phone and that was it. I was sitting in the booth like, 'Oh my God, I feel so different.' I felt like I had lost a thousand pounds, like I had been chained down so long, and it was freedom." Later that day his sister called. Big Ivan was dead. His suffering was over. In forgiveness, it seemed, his chains had also been broken.

After that day, Ryan was a different man. He doubled down his commitment to everything he was doing. His mood leveled and the good news kept coming. He moved into his own apartment off campus. He finished his probation and his record was expunged. One day, during the holidays, he called his now seventeen-year-old daughter to ask what she wanted him to send for Christmas. Her answer floored him. "All I want is to pick you up from the airport."

"What do you mean?" he said.

"I talked to my mother. She said we could see each other. I got a car. I can pick you up myself," she told her father.

I can remember the moment he ran into my office, every bit the excited child on Christmas morning. "My daughter wants to see me! They said I could see my daughter!"

"Calm down, calm down," I told him. But I could barely keep calm myself. We got him a ticket. Soon enough, Ryan was boarding his first plane ever to see the daughter he hadn't seen since she was a toddler.

Then one day Ryan walked into my office again. He was carrying a folder full of documents, and he asked me to sit at the conference table for a few minutes. With an authority in his voice that was new to me, he began to tell me about the chapter of his life he had just finished writing.

Ryan had decided, on his own, to go through training to become a certified security officer. He had taken multiple classes, passed many exams, and successfully made his way through the firearm tests (this time in legal fashion)—all on his own. Certification in hand, he had started his own security company, an LLC (yes, he had saved his money and gotten the help of a lawyer), and he named it Watchmen Protective Services. He already had contracts in place, officers hired and trained, and positive cash flow. His years of working at City of Refuge, during which he had calmly navigated both a shooting and a tornado on campus, had made him uniquely qualified to provide security to homeless shelters. He had approached them with exactly that pitch, and he had five contracts in a month.

This conversation with Ryan happened in the dark period after Jake's death, when the weight of all the people whom we kept lifting after another fall felt impossibly heavy. Sitting in amazement, I sensed that weight beginning to lift just a bit. Ryan explained that he had realized some months earlier that he had become dependent on City of Refuge and me and that he was leaning on us rather than walking on his own. He knew we would help him if he shared his dream about becoming certified and owning a company, but he had decided to do it without our help because he wanted us to think well of him and to be proud of him. The weight lessened a bit more.

His story finished, Ryan closed the folder and sat back in his chair, a look of accomplishment and achievement on his face. Yet I could see that something was still missing and that the puzzle had not been quite completed. I was looking at a man who once led robberies and inflicted pain on innocent people, a man who had spent many days locked up. Suddenly the revelation of what was missing came to me like a lightning bolt from a stormy sky. I leaned toward Ryan, picked up the folder of information, and simply said, "I am proud of you." Tears pooled in his eyes and escaped down a face that had not seen nearly enough smiles. Now a smile as wide as Kansas broke out. He stood, shook my hand, and said, "I knew I could make you proud." He strode confidently out of my office.

Now Ryan transforms others. He got his instructor's license and started offering free training for the homeless community in a local park—guys he had met at City of Refuge who said, "Train and hire *us*!" When our Workforce Innovation Hub opened, we invited Ryan to operate the security training school there to provide skills training and to mentor folks through the challenges that keep them from working. In 2018, Watchman Protective Services was three years old and had expanded to thirty employees working contracts all over Atlanta.

WHAT RYAN HAS ACCOMPLISHED is remarkable, but I'm happy to say that almost everyone we work with redirects the energy once consumed by addiction and misery into helping others. Vanessa, for example. Every time she's been physically able, she has been a volunteer on our campus, at her own request. For a long time, she assumed the role of lunch lady and had sole responsibility for preparing and packing three hundred sack lunches a day to be distributed around town. She would set up camp at a sixty-inch round table where she would arrange the items needed for lunch in order, starting on her left. First, a large stack of sandwich bread, followed by containers of turkey or ham, then came cheese, mustard, another stack of sandwich bread, plastic sandwich baggies, brown bags, bottled water, fruit, and chips.

She was proud to be seen sitting at the table packing lunches; this was her job and her way of giving back to the place that had saved her life. She became extremely territorial about it, refusing offers of help. Her concentration in preparing these lunches was so great that I'd sometimes see a little drool of dip juice run down her chin—but I swear, it never would drop to the table below.

Tennie Woods is another contributor whose light shines

bright. Tennie grew up in a housing project twenty minutes from City of Refuge. When her husband—her childhood sweetheart and best friend for decades—passed away from cancer, she was devastated and turned to alcohol and marijuana to dull the pain. She started dealing cocaine to support her marijuana habit, but dealing turned into using. "It got where I didn't care if somebody did come and buy it, because I was turning out to be my best customer," she says. Neither jail stints nor drug recovery programs seemed to make a difference. Her path once released was always the same: cigarettes, then beer, then finding someone who would let her sell. "Once you're in it for a while, you stop having feelings, you know? Normal feelings, like compassion," she says now.

She got more and more tired as the months passed, and finally one day she decided she was done with this life that was draining her soul. In the middle of a busy sales day, she told everybody in the house to get out. She called the cops and went out to the porch. She took the clip out of her .25 automatic and put it to one side of her. To the other, she put her drugs and her pipe. Then she waited. Thirty minutes she sat there without budging until finally the cops came, and she put her hands up. She slowly, calmly followed every instruction they gave her.

"You're the most cooperative suspect that we've picked up in a long time," they said, not quite believing it could be so easy. They hesitated in front of the house, her wrists in cuffs.

"I'm tired. I'm ready," she told them. "What's the holdup?"

They asked if she needed to lock the doors to her house.

"It don't belong to me no way," she said.

A new judge sentenced her to the same drug program as before. This time, she was dropped off at City of Refuge from Fulton County Jail. We were to provide a safe place for her to stay while she did her eighteen months of Drug Court. She started volunteering in the kitchen and around the property. Eventually she moved into House of Shechem, with Vanessa.

From day one, Tennie was in charge of her own transformation. But we were glad to be the place where she could safely explore a new life. Now she stands strong enough to take care of others. In 2008, we needed a full-time security guard to work nights at Eden Village. Tennie was now living off campus with Vanessa, and she had been working part time with us for some months. Since the first day she had been dropped off on our campus, she had been nothing but grateful and respectful, dedicated to doing the work to make each day better. She had been sober now for years, faithfully attending weekly AA meetings. I couldn't think of a better candidate for permanent, full-time employment.

I called her up and offered her the job. "Yes, sir. Whatever you need, Bruce," is what she said on the phone at the time. When I asked her about that call more recently, she told me more. "Chills went over me. Once I got off that phone, I'm telling you, it was like I felt something from here down. It changed my whole life," she says.

Today, Tennie works specifically with women on campus who have escaped lives as victims of sex trafficking. "When certain ladies come in, I can look at them and tell before they even tell me anything about them, about where they've been, what they've done, what they've been though," says Tennie. "I can relate to them about the drugs and the alcohol and the prostitution. I never prostituted—these were the same kind of ladies I used and abused. To now be able to show them some love and my strength and hope for them, it's healing." In 2017, we announced Tennie as employee of the year at the annual holiday party. The following year, she hit her ten-year anniversary of working with us.

Tennie clocks out at seven every morning. She goes to pick up her three-year-old grandson, whom she keeps until lunch. Then she takes care of herself and gets some rest. Every day, she chats with her sister, who, with Tennie's help, went clean two years ago and is now moving into her own apartment. On weekends, she attends an AA meeting. You can often find her in our gym, shooting ball. The rest of the time she spends protecting the women of City of Refuge.

Most everyone in our program likes me or at least respects me. But at the end of the day, I'm still an outsider. That's one reason why the gifts of people like Ryan, Tennie,

Greg, and so many others are critical to what we do. Our residents know I've never been addicted to crack cocaine or heroin. They know alcohol never controlled my life, and in spite of the arrest warrant I keep in my desk drawer, I've never done hard time. They know the only times I slept outside were nights I chose to camp out in my nice waterproof tent. Twenty-one years in, I'm still a bit of a curiosity: Ghetto Rev, the white guy from the mountains hanging out in a neighborhood whose residents are almost exclusively people of color.

And so, leader or not, there are times that I need to step back. I need my friends with stories and backgrounds different from mine to step forward, make decisions, and lead others to better days. It's easy to do because in one way, the most important way, we are exactly alike: We all believe we're doing the most satisfying, dignified work we could ever know.

CHAPTER 10

Changing Names, Changing Lives

One thing you can't hide / Is when you're crippled inside.
—JOHN LENNON, "CRIPPLED INSIDE"

When I think about our journey at City of Refuge, I am amazed as anybody else at what has been built on a simple foundation of trust. But what's truly amazing isn't my trust or the trust of any volunteer. It's the awesomely radical trust that the people we help are so often able to discover. When they first arrive, years of bad experiences, sometimes a lifetime, have robbed many of the belief that someone's open palm is not there to slap them down but to pull them to safety. And yet, whether slowly or quickly, always on their own time line, so many learn to trust us. They learn to trust others. And they learn to trust themselves and the possibility that the things they do today will lead to rewards tomorrow.

I've had the honor to watch hundreds of people bloom

into a new relationship with themselves and their potential. And yet nothing and no one in our history prepared me for the journeys of courage I would witness when we decided to create a home for women who had escaped sex trafficking.

"I NEED YOU *to take me downtown to the courthouse and wipe away the fact that I ever existed. I need my name changed, my Social Security number changed, and a new birth certificate. We have to change everything or they will find me and they will kill me.*"

Her words, spoken with a trembling voice and through tears, shocked me. I had met Michelle a few weeks earlier after a friend of mine from another state called to say they had encountered a young woman who had escaped from sex trafficking and needed a place to hide away until she was ready to engage in a program of restorative care. We sent someone to pick her up and they drove random routes back to Atlanta, watching the rearview mirror constantly to see if they were being followed. Michelle lay in the back seat, sleeping for a few moments at a time and weeping the rest of the time.

When she arrived on campus I escorted her to her room in our housing center and let her know that we would take care of her for as long as she needed. Nodding slightly, she crawled into bed, pulled the comforter up to her chin, and turned her face toward the wall without speaking a word. That's where

Michelle stayed for a month—under that comforter, facing that wall. We delivered food to her room and she came out only to visit the bathroom and shower periodically. I instructed my staff to leave her alone even though she was not abiding by the rules of the program. Somehow I knew that whatever she had experienced, it had wounded her to the core of her being. I was not going to force her to do anything until she was ready. The day my staff informed me she wanted to see me was a day that broke my heart, shook my world, and changed my approach to confronting the brutal reality of human trafficking.

City of Refuge was well established at this point. The building was 100 percent free of rats. More than a thousand women a year were exchanging homelessness for loving care at Eden Village, our kitchen was turning out hundreds of thousands of hot meals, and a first class had graduated from our new auto mechanic training program. Volunteers and donors were investing millions of dollars and hundreds of thousands of hours to our organization. Recognition had come in many forms and we had settled into the regular routine of raising money, hiring staff, enhancing programs, and birthing hope.

By this time, most of the people in the neighborhood had accepted us, and the violent encounters and thievery were far fewer than in the past. While my daughters still knew not to turn left when leaving the property, Rhonda and I felt confident that the girls knew the signs of danger and were proactive in being wise as they traveled in and out of the community.

Our housing program was operating at max capacity. The medical clinic was overflowing with people needing care. Youth and children were being served well, and it was as though the torrent of need for compassion and care had slowed to a steady flow of cool, fresh water. It wasn't that there were fewer people in need; we just had more hands and hearts to help them. Staying afloat was manageable almost every day. Then Michelle asked to see me.

Life presents all of us with moments. Some of those moments require nothing of us other than to be present, whether with joy or sorrow. Other moments require some action, a bit of movement, or the reexamination of some belief we once felt sure of. Then there are moments that shake us, challenge us, confront us. They do not allow us to simply abide them or walk away from them but will leave us with an indelible mark. They force us to make a decision that will either radically change our lives or leave us wondering what could have been. These crucible moments do not come along very often; I expect each of us will have only a few. But when we see one coming, we know immediately that the moment is going to cost us greatly, whatever we choose.

Listening to Michelle was such a moment. The desperation in her voice frightened me more than any of the encounters I had experienced with guys from the street who had threatened my life. The tone of her voice and the look in her eye, along with her weeks of silent convalescence, convinced me she was telling the absolute truth. Someone was looking for her, and if they found her, they would kill her. Nothing I had done to that point, nothing I had organized, built, or experienced had fully prepared me for the absolute sense of terror Michelle brought to our conversation. An awakening had taken place in her mind and a realization had grabbed her. She could not stay in our bed in our building for the rest of her life, and if she left, they would be waiting for her someplace at some time.

"Will you do that, Mr. Bruce, will you take me to the courthouse? Can we go today? Can we go now? I'll get ready really fast. Let's go, please, let's go now," she said. I was standing up but felt as though I was falling down, losing my balance emotionally. What should I do? My relationship with Michelle covered all of ten minutes—five minutes when I walked her into the space for the first time and five now as I listened to her pleas for a new identity.

"Okay," I said, "let's talk about this for a minute. I am glad to help you but I need to understand why you want to change your name, why you are afraid, and who you think will kill you."

Wringing her hands, eyes darting about, she shared her story with me. We've all heard nightmarish things second-hand or in the news, but hearing a person's story face-to-face, without any filter to slow the flow of raw emotion, is a different deal altogether. I can't share all the details, as the story involved people in positions of power, legal authorities, and others that you would never believe could be involved in the sale of a twenty-one-year-old girl, resulting in her being locked in a facility where her only human contact, day and night, was by men who were there to rape and assault her.

For more than three years this had been her life, or better stated, her existence. Finally, with the understanding that she might die, she used a broken piece of the bed frame to shatter a small window high above her place of horrors. Using strength she did not know she possessed, she pulled herself up, and contorting her body in painful ways, squeezed through the opening, falling several feet to the ground below. Though covered in cuts and bruises from broken window glass and her subsequent fall, she muffled her cries of pain and ran and ran and ran without looking back a single time.

She told the story in detail, but strangely enough, the deeper she dove into it the more she became detached and emotionless. She stopped wringing her hands and her eyes focused on mine. It was as though she was on the outside looking in at someone else's story. The coping mechanism that we all have deep within us activated, and in a move to protect her own heart, she became devoid of emotion. As her personality changed, my level of fear actually increased.

At City of Refuge we deal daily with anger, tears, frustration, and the like. It's just the way things are. Those things no longer knock me off my path. In fact, anxiety sets in only when a few days pass in relative quietude. This time with

Michelle was something different. Many people came to us to separate themselves from their old life and build a healthier identity before returning. This was the first time I had ever met someone who had escaped from a nightmare so extreme, so out of her control, that her former identity needed to be annihilated to move forward.

I was not prepared. The emotional loss of balance manifested itself physically and I found myself sitting on the bed beside Michelle, holding her hand, saying nothing. I'm not sure how long we sat there before I spoke.

"Be ready in the morning and I will have one of the ladies on staff take you to the courthouse and we will do whatever is necessary to change your name and wipe away your past."

"I think it costs money," she replied.

"Don't worry about the money; just be ready in the morning." I stood and she pulled the comforter up to her chin and turned to face the wall.

I walked the long hallway to my office, already making plans regarding the home we would build for ladies like Michelle who had been trafficked and exploited. In that moment I knew that there would be no debate, no discussion, no request for board approval as to whether or not we would build the house and develop the program. That moment with Michelle changed who I was, and it would now change what City of Refuge was. We were adding a new mission.

I am sure I had offered prayers in the past for victims of

trafficking, or had donated money here or there to the cause, but for the most part I was oblivious to these victims. I, as most do, had simply thrown a little bit of who I was and what I possessed at something that was far darker than I realized, and by doing so I had massaged my conscience just enough to keep moving while ignoring the *thing* staring me in the face. I now had visceral evidence that sexual slavery existed in the United States of America. Come hell, high water, push-back, risk, or any other obstacle that may arise, I committed to myself while walking from Michelle's room to my office that we would be a part of the process of healing and resto-ration for precious human beings like Michelle.

Sitting at my desk I began to make notes regarding where the house would be, how many bedrooms it would have, how many women we could care for daily, the number of staff we would need, what a budget for such a house would look like. My notes covered a couple pages of paper when it struck me—I knew nothing about the sex-trafficking industry, ab-solutely nothing. City of Refuge was already a major player in the disruption of poverty, but meeting the needs of sex-trafficking victims represented a completely new challenge for us. I had no understanding of the scope—the number of victims, the impact to communities, the long-term conse-quences. I didn't have a profile of traffickers or pimps other than what I had seen in a movie or on the corner down the street. Obviously, there is a process of grooming and recruiting, but how does that happen? What role does poverty play? What about drug addiction?

Those were among dozens of questions I had no answers for. If we were going to be in the space, we would need to be educated and informed about the space. I slumped a bit in my chair as my thoughts began to career through my mind like an out-of-control train, crashing into walls of logic and limitation. If I had to research in order to become informed and educated, and had to attend training sessions and seminars before launching the program and building the house, a significant amount of time would pass, and with each passing day, another woman like Michelle would be without a safe place to stay where healing and restoration could happen.

I'm just not wired to wait; I'm wired to do. So I called the two or three places in my city that I knew provided space for victims and inquired regarding availability. Every place I called had a waiting list. I sent messages to my circle of friends asking about their knowledge of such places. No one could provide me with a list. It was becoming clear that existing support services were inadequate to meet the level of need. So I went back to my notepad and resumed writing. While I completely understand that others will take issue (and have taken issue) with my approach, I decided that we would learn on the go, with all the help we could find, just like always. Surely meeting urgent needs imperfectly was better than not meeting them at all.

We transported Michelle to and from the courthouse, paid the fees, and filed the paperwork for her name and Social Security changes. A few days later she received her new documents and quickly settled into a completely new identity with change of hair color, different style of clothing, and, I am sure, a different view of life. As our new home was not yet completed, we referred Michelle to a partner agency that runs long-term recovery homes. She was accepted and moved on as a new person. We lost touch with her and I have no idea how she fared in the program or what life looks like for her today. I do know that she inspired me to do something I had never before considered, and that inspiration meant City of Refuge would embark on a journey that no one on our team had planned to travel.

TELLING STORIES and raising money happen to be two things I do well. I now threw myself at both with a lot of passion and energy. I assigned staff members the task of gathering data, building reports, and writing case statements—the beginning of our education as an organization in this new mission. I told stories and raised money. Gifts came in all shapes and sizes, ranging from very small amounts to amounts that amazed me. We needed a million dollars to build and furnish the anti-trafficking space, as well as additional dollars to cover operational expenses in the first year, so I told stories and asked for money. We needed building plans and interior designs, so I told stories and asked for those plans and designs to be donated without cost. And they were.

While building the physical space was expensive, I knew it would be the easy part. The bigger challenge was how to care for the survivors who would recover there. Flashing back to the shell-shocked month Michelle spent in the cocoon of her sheets, I grasped the enormity of the task. We reached out to successful organizations and asked for best practices, curriculum, and guidance. I'd love to say that the responses we received were all helpful and that everyone we spoke to expressed a desire to work together, but that's not what happened. Several agencies expressed disappointment that City of Refuge would enter this space. They implied, or even said, that we should continue to do what we had been doing and leave the trafficking and exploitation issue to them. They were not too different from Vanessa lording it over her bag lunches—except unlike Vanessa they couldn't make enough lunches. None of them had had beds to offer me for Michelle. Their attitude puzzled me. Rather than try to understand why good people were more focused on guarding their crisis fiefdom than they were on expanding resources for women in need, I decided to plow ahead.

Not everyone wanted to hear the story of Michelle and others like her. Sex trafficking, rape, sexual abuse, branding of women, and the like do not make for good dinner conversation. (Reactions are even worse when I speak about male trafficking victims, a group we hope to turn our attention to next.) I was often asked to "tone down" my description of the violence perpetrated on the victims and to be a bit more delicate in my approach to making people aware of the issue and the consequences associated with it. I was not about to let some donor or politician or pastor tell me to ease up on the story. The story was what it was and it had to be told just as it was.

I went to foundations, corporations, and individuals, and almost no one said no. It took about a year, but we raised the $1 million and built the house. I hired an interior designer, and I told her that I wanted every woman to feel loved, cared for, and affirmed as they entered the building. She responded with warm colors on the walls, beautiful furniture and bedding, bathrobes and slippers for every resident. A beautifully appointed common area served as the gathering spot, and meals were served around a large, rustic dining room table where everyone was considered family.

Soon we welcomed our first ten women to the home we had built them, and it was a deeply emotional experience for everyone involved. Case managers began meeting with the women and trauma-informed care was implemented. Counseling was part of the daily routine and drug addiction programs were initiated for those who needed them. Therapy included group sessions as well as individualized life plans.

We quickly understood that it would not suffice to operate as a safe house only. We would need to add a long-term component to our plans. This would mean many more dollars would have to be raised, requiring the telling of many more stories. Over time, one house and ten beds became forty beds in four houses. As of 2018, more than five hundred women have resided in our restoration homes. A large percentage of them successfully completed the program and moved on to places of stability and productivity. Others lost their way, their painful histories still dominating their thoughts, telling them lies they were powerless to dispute.

LONG AGO I stopped trying to figure out whether a lady would succeed or fail. Attempts to do so revealed only how poor a predictor I was. Many ladies who I thought had no chance at success are now well past their struggles and are living productive lives. Many others I thought would thrive in our environment lost the will to battle on. I still have no idea how one returns to those places of pain, but since I have not experienced their hardship, I cannot judge.

Not a chance she's going to make it, I remember thinking the first time I met Stephanie. I doubt if a form of rock has been discovered that is harder than Stephanie seemed the first time I met her. Passing by her in the hallway left me feeling a chill. She did not speak and avoided eye contact at all cost, turning her head as needed so as not to accidentally look my way. Men frightened her, and it didn't take a private investigator to discover that she had good reason to hate all of them. As I learned her story I started to better understand her behavior.

Stephanie was born into a family that was part of a cult. She was reared in a culture that thought it was acceptable to traffic their daughters as an enterprise to generate the funding needed to support the group as they traveled the country. They moved every few weeks to avoid detection by legal authorities. Stephanie had been raped in hotels, homes, vehicles, and the boxcars of trains. She had witnessed unbelievable abuse inflicted on her siblings and friends and had been the victim many times of that same abuse.

Stephanie's abuse began when she was five years old. Eighteen years later she finally got up the nerve to escape. She "borrowed" a pickup truck and drove to Atlanta, where she didn't know a soul. Some might call it luck, but I call it providence. Either way, Stephanie met some people who knew about our program and she was soon residing in our safe house. Being off the streets and in our home was wonderful, but Stephanie was not quite ready for the structure, guidelines, and protocols of the house. Simple words or expressions or sounds could serve as triggers leading to violent eruptions of emotion.

The opinion of the majority of the house staff was that

Stephanie should be admitted to a mental health institution in an effort to gain control of her emotions and to address her detachment disorder. I agreed with the program director that hospitalization and medication were not the solution in this particular case. Unconditional love and acceptance—things Stephanie had never experienced—seemed to be a better treatment plan, so we decided she could stay as long as necessary.

Were there days I questioned our decision to allow Stephanie to stay? Does the earth orbit around the sun? Of course I questioned that decision. I questioned the decision when she shattered the double-paned glass of the house door. I questioned that decision when she ran out of the house and down the street with the program director in hot pursuit. I questioned that decision when she slammed doors, cursed at staff, threw items, and curled up into a ball on the floor, closed to the world around her for hours at a time. But I didn't change the decision, since love and acceptance were still the answer. I was convinced of it—and even surer that trust would take seed with time, if we could just be patient enough.

And slowly, ever so slowly, like blades of grass making their way out of frozen soil, a softer side of Stephanie began to emerge. Now and then she would glance at me in the hallway and a whisper of "hello" would fall from her lips. These small things were actually huge victories and not one of them was taken for granted. A more gentle disposition revealed itself, day by day. Fewer things were being broken, fewer insults thrown, and she began to cooperate with her case workers and roommates. Stephanie started to show up for times of worship and engage in singing. She would even respond to invitations for prayer and dialogue.

The story that had been told over and over, and the dollars that had been raised, were now paying off in the most dramatic ways, and we were witnessing it firsthand. Months passed and Stephanie and I became friends from a distance. Little by little she would talk to me and a smile would come to her face when she saw me. Day by day, she was learning trust—living testimony that the human heart is strong enough, and hungry enough, to overcome even the most brutal mistreatment and return to love.

Wind River Ranch in Colorado is absolutely beautiful. Set between two mountain ranges, it could match any American Masters landscape. Rustic cabins dot the land and a log dining hall serves as gathering grounds for staff and visitors. Horses roam the pasture and a crew of wranglers make sure barn operations run smoothly. The ranch is a place where families and individuals go to escape the troubles of life for a few days, a place to relax, refresh, and be renewed. Rhonda, the girls, and I have been privileged to spend several weeks there over the past few years, and it is one of our favorite places.

The director of the ranch came to visit City of Refuge while Stephanie was living with us. Moved by the stories I shared and the folks he met, he committed then and there to raise enough money to host a couple dozen of our survivors for a week at the ranch. Loving a big adventure, I immediately declared that I would raise the money for airline tickets, along with boots, jeans, and Western shirts for all the ladies. We both went to work and soon had the money to pull off this grand event.

When the day came, several of my staff boarded the plane with a group of residents from our program and left Atlanta headed for Denver. From there they drove to Estes Park and enjoyed a wonderful week of great food, devotional time, group therapy, and horseback riding. To this day, many of them say it was one of the highlights of their life. The last day of their trip was a Friday, and on Thursday I boarded a flight for Denver, rented a car, and headed toward the ranch. I'd seen before that small gestures can have a huge impact on people who are coming out of crisis environments. With this in mind, I made a stop in town to purchase enough flowers and chocolate for every woman there to receive more than she needed. The gifts were frivolous, but these particular frivolous gifts are still cultural milestones, and those milestones matter.

I had contacted friends from California who were musicians and vocalists, and they flew in and met me at the ranch. A five-star meal was being prepared as the final dinner of the trip, and ranch staff were standing ready to serve the ladies as though they were royalty. My friends began playing the piano and singing as the ladies drifted into the dining hall. As each entered, I greeted them and handed them my gifts and simply said, "I love you." They were not expecting my visit, and the memory of the looks on their faces brings me to tears even now. In that moment, I was their surrogate father, brother, or boyfriend—in contrast with the past, a positive, loving male figure who demanded nothing of them. Not so long ago in these women's lives, a man's attention had been only a thing of terror. Now things were different. They were different. My attention, marked with gifts, had become a re-flection of their strength and bravery.

Stephanie was among the last to enter. I was very nervous about how she would react to seeing me there with gifts for her. She still had never been close enough to touch my hand held at arm's length, so I feared reaching out even to receive flowers might trigger an outburst. Stephanie opened the door and stepped into the dining hall. My friends were singing the song "You Are So Beautiful," and the candles were burning on the dining room tables. Eyes darted back and forth be-tween Stephanie and me, and those who knew her story held their breath, anxious to see her response. A huge smile burst on her face and she ran to me, jumping into my arms and nearly knocking me down. (Stephanie was an adult, but often very childlike in her behavior; her first abuse occurred at such a young age, it seemed to have stunted her emotional and cognitive development.) Gaining her balance, she took the roses and chocolate, leaned in and kissed me on the cheek and said boldly, "I love you, Pastor Bruce." As she skipped away to her table, she looked back and mouthed, "Thank you." Stunned, I picked up the next set of gifts and turned to greet the woman entering the room.

Following dessert we gathered at the farmhouse around a fire blazing in a huge stone pit. We sang more songs, shed some tears, and shared some laughter. The week of escape was about to conclude and everyone was hanging on to the last few moments of reprieve from the world they had left but would now return to. Stephanie stood and asked to speak. "Just before dinner I went over by the big tree on the other side of the dining hall and spent some time alone. While I was there I decided to pray. 'God,' I said, 'if you are real, I'd like to ask you for a favor. I'd like to hear a man say he loves me just because he loves me and not because he wants something from me. And, God, if you don't mind, I'd like that man to be someone that reminds me of Pastor Bruce.'"

The distance between this Stephanie and the one I had met months before was stunning. I was completely humbled.

"Well, when I opened the door to the dining hall, Pastor Bruce was standing there with flowers and chocolate and he looked at me and told me he loved me. It wasn't someone who reminded me of Pastor Bruce, it actually *was* Pastor Bruce. I just want all y'all to know, I believe there is a God now and I believe He cares about me."

I drove back to Denver that night and checked into a

hotel room. Emotionally exhausted, I fell asleep. The next morning I boarded a plane back to Atlanta, drove to the office, and began the work of setting more appointments to tell the story while developing the strategy to raise even more money.

Stephanie approached staff members a few weeks after returning home from Colorado and expressed her desire to have her name changed—not because she was afraid someone would kill her, though they might, but simply because she had decided it was time to embrace a new life, a new identity, and a new perspective. It seemed that her new dignity and self-esteem left no space for her old self. We took her to the courthouse and helped her complete the paperwork. We paid the fees and wiped away the fact that Stephanie ever existed. Victoria Hope would now be her name, marking this new existence built on love, trust, and acceptance.

Our work continues. We've increased from ten bedrooms to thirty-four and have both a safe house and long-term trauma-informed care. Over five years, we've been part of the restoration process for more than seven hundred women.

CHAPTER 11

Trust + Time = Transformation

The race is not always to the swift,
but to those who keep on moving.

—ECCLESIASTES 9:11

We have so little control over life or the lives of the people we care most about. But we can never love or trust less because of it. At 3:05 a.m. on Sunday, May 14, 2017, death came for Cecil Deel, my giant of a father. The doctors had given him eighteen months to live, but we got only three. In his last days, as I picked him up from his recliner to carry him to the table for a meal or to the restroom, he would playfully pat me on the head and tell me he was glad I was strong enough to carry him.

It was my dad who first etched unwavering trust into my being and served as my life's model for how to help inspire it in others. I am well aware of the moments of disappointment I brought him, but he never once expressed it. In the years after college when I considered a secular profession, he didn't question or judge me, even though I knew he'd hoped I'd follow him into ministry. He let me know he was there for counsel if I wanted it, but otherwise he stepped back to let me find my way. He was always the lead cheerleader on the sidelines of my existence, bragging about everything from my ability to play ball to how well I cared for my family. His greatest disappointment was leaving this world before my mother, who has advanced Alzheimer's. He wanted to care for her until she passed.

Many start strong but few finish well. The work of City of Refuge has seen a multitude of staff and volunteers come and go. Their hearts of compassion drew them to us but the daily emotional drain eventually led them away. I hold no hard feelings toward any of those who gave up in the middle of changing the world. I know personally that the world can sometimes kick us in the gut until the breath simply gives way to the pain.

My father was the man who showed me how to finish well. Finishing well means never giving up, pure and simple. It means staying tirelessly committed to your goal and never being deterred by anyone else's judgment of what is the "right" outcome.

As I mentioned earlier, Dad was a preacher, pastor, and missionary. It was clear to all who met him that he was fully committed to the calling for which he absolutely believed he had been created. The problem for me, as a teenager and then a young man, was that the spiritual rewards to himself and others were hard to grasp. What I *could* see were the very tangible challenges of the way my dad chose to live his life. Money was always scarce, and he would often have to work two or more jobs just to make ends meet. People he was trying to serve often turned on him, and he was asked to leave churches where he had ruffled the feathers of old-timers who possessed too much power and not enough grace. We moved often, and leaving behind friends and familiarity never got easier. My dad's calling took him to the Philippines, where he served for a number of years, and that meant that he, my mom, and my little sister were not with us when Rhonda and I got married. I clearly remember resenting my dad's calling, spending days being angry that he was chasing his destiny, days of feeling frustrated because his work often seemed to be in vain. But years after his official retirement, he was still working with the same conviction and energy.

CECIL DEEL NEVER QUIT. He never even talked about quitting and, as far as I know, never considered quitting. This became even clearer to me in the final weeks of his life, when my brothers, Jeff and Keith, and my sister, April, and I spent quality hours with Dad and listened as he recounted stories of his childhood and early adulthood, many of which I had never heard before. He told me about going AWOL from the military, and then getting arrested and serving time. I knew that history, but I was more surprised to hear how hard it was for him to reenter normal life and to establish himself in the ministry with that black mark on his record. It was hard, but he did it. He talked about his father. When my dad decided to become a pastor, his alcoholic, anti-religious father told him never to come home again. But my father never gave up. Later in life, he renewed their relationship through a long series of visits and conversations—always gentle, always patient, never judging. By the time his father passed away, they were extremely close. As with everything in his life, he believed nothing ever had a final answer—the only answer was to keep trying and see what happened. When I was seven or eight years old and twenty-one shots were fired into our house by an angry man whose abused wife had taken sanctuary with our family, my dad didn't quit. When the message of grace and peace that he preached both with his words and his life was rejected by the listeners, he didn't quit. Neither prayers unanswered nor dreams unrealized convinced him to quit. He simply stayed the course, believed the best was yet to come, and loved on people along the way.

As the hearse carrying my father's body left his home around 6:30 a.m. that painful morning of his death, the sun had just started its ascent into the sky and it was as though the earth was awakening at that very moment. The birds that Dad so enjoyed listening to as he sat on the front porch of his home shook off their own slumber and began to sing a beautiful melody as the hearse drove away. Dad had finished well, and I understood my assignment in a more profound way than at any point in the past twenty years.

TOO OFTEN, we define success by the outcomes that *others* decide are important, which usually boils down to those that are most easily measurable. It's the same mistake I once made in evaluating my father's contributions to the world. Instead of recognizing the gratitude and relief of those he ministered to, I was counting heads and judging his lack of status or reward.

When you run a nonprofit, outcome-based measurements are required to receive funding from foundations. Projections related to the number of lives you will save, people you will put to work, and dollars you will keep in the government's coffers rather than having them spent on people who are incarcerated or admitted to a mental health facility are often the measuring sticks for approval. Society wants numbers, and faces to go with those numbers, in order to validate the work of people and organizations that are attempting to help men, women, and families escape life on the margin.

Chasing scant resources, organizations spend an inordinate amount of time counting the number of meals served, the number of beds occupied, the number of kids who graduate. Of course, we do this ourselves, so that I can readily trot out facts such as "Eden Village created $65.6 million in economic impact in 2016. One-hundred thirty-nine women graduated into stable employment. Based on historical numbers, 80 percent of these women will maintain employment beyond the first year with projected twenty-year earnings of $591,765." We need accountability for the money we're spending and for the precious lives who are placed in our care. We all want positive outcomes and data to help improve every aspect of what we do.

But there is so much that the numbers utterly fail to capture. Returning dignity to a single human life is immeasurable and not always accompanied by the outcomes that society wants to rubber-stamp. If all we worked for were those "true stories of incredible transformation" that make for nice brochures and lead to people writing us big checks, so much would be lost.

Eden Village, still our bedrock program, is six months long. That's enough time for many residents to graduate into stable lives—and we happily, greedily tally them up. For others, six months is just the beginning of their healing journey. If trust is the first essential resource for transformation, time is the second, and it is a wide-ranging variable.

Take Rufus. It was years into our relationship before his profanity-laden tirades abated and his drug and alcohol use started a steady decline. Every now and then we started to see smiles, or even hear a "thank you" when he picked up a plate of food or received a warm jacket. Every moment of peace and civility was documented with great fanfare. I don't think I would be overstating things to say that even the small changes in Rufus's behavior, let alone the big ones, were so exhilarating that they motivated our team of staff and volunteers to work even harder. *If Rufus can change, anyone can change* was a thought that seemed to take root and create momentum in a good direction. Eight years into our labor, one of those we had silently thought would never get it right was suddenly on the edge of "getting it right."

After a decade in our care, he made the ultimate leap. At the time, he was still on and off drugs and alcohol. After one binge, he woke to a symptom he'd never had; he was having trouble focusing his eyes. In that moment, what he'd later learn was diabetes was a terrifying unknown. He called his best friend, Steve Grimes.

"If you come get me, this be it," he told Steve. "I'll never look back."

Steve was immediately by his side. While in our care, Rufus enrolled in AA, which helped him achieve what no prior detox program (and there were many) had been able to. He hasn't had alcohol or drugs since. Eventually he quit nicotine, too. He had been smoking since he was eleven, but he didn't let that stop him from going cold turkey. "I said that's it. No slowin' down. Did it. Boom," he says. He never smoked again.

Rufus today lives in a house furnished by City of Refuge. We have paid the rent and utilities and have provided Rufus with food and clothing for more than ten years. (With transportation, too: Rufus's loyal friend Steve has an unpaid second job as his personal chauffeur, since Rufus feels public transportation puts him too close to the riffraff.) Rufus is one of a couple dozen people we've supported similarly, finding the funding on a case-by-case basis. When help beyond our established programs is needed, we never say no. We sometimes say "not yet"—then race to find the money.

Rufus spent months working with our staff to complete his paperwork for Social Security Disability support, no easy task for someone with a fourth-grade education. Accomplishing that was a very proud moment. In 2018, he got his first check—and he immediately started giving back. Every single week, he gets cash from the bank, puts it in an envelope, writes City of Refuge on it, and hand delivers it to me. In his words, "You can take my little piece of money and help somebody else who is living like I used to. You can help them like you helped me and you sure did help me. I wouldn't be alive if you hadn't shown up in my world."

In many ways Rufus does not meet the criteria set by

society for success. He is still dependent on others and, due to chronic health issues, will never work a regular job. He can't drive and, despite early enthusiasm and effort, has been unable to earn his GED. In our world, however, Rufus is an incredible success. He no longer suffers under the omnipresent danger of life as a sex worker. He no longer steals to support a drug habit. He is free from alcoholism and heroin addiction. Rufus has not stabbed or beaten anyone in more than a decade. He shows up every Sunday at our little church and engages in a worship experience that brings him great joy. There and at City of Refuge, Rufus is embraced, affirmed, and loved in ways most people will never experience in their lives.

Rufus is as stable as anyone can expect considering the abuse he suffered as a child and the more than twenty-five years he lived on the streets of our city. Each day is a victory. He says, "Even today I battle with the thoughts in my head. But my words, I don't act on." He now has to use a walker to get around because his right knee aches all the time as a result of being run over by the angry customer he tried to rob. Diabetes is taking its toll, and junk food is a stubborn last addiction. Yet he smiles and he tells folks at City of Refuge that he loves them. He has positive relationships with his brother and sister, and he visits them in Florida. His weekly envelope of small bills is as valuable to me as our richest donor's check.

———

"TRANSFORMATION" shouldn't be misunderstood as something you do once and then are finished with. We all have periods in our life when we lose our way or need to be carried by people who love us. Vanessa recently completed a second tour as a resident in our women's transitional program. She had lived several years on her own, but health and mental challenges dictated a move back to the place where it all started a dozen years ago. Barely able to get around, she spends most of her days sitting at a table in Eden Village, looking out the window to see who was walking across the parking lot of our campus on that particular day. Her favorite thing is still a gum full of snuff, and when she happens to run out, she becomes one of the more cantankerous people you've ever been around.

Vanessa can no longer control her bladder and has to wear adult diapers. She was initially deeply embarrassed and secretive about her problem, so we made sure the diapers were taken to her room in a nondescript package. The cleaning crew removed the trash in her room more frequently than in other rooms in order to keep her living space as fresh as possible. She can't manage her money, so my staff withdraws her funds at the beginning of each month and gives her a certain amount each week. We've done this for many folks for a short period of time as they transition to full in-dependence; Vanessa is the only one for whom we've done it for ten years, because she needs and wants the help (most of the time, anyway). She knows that with total control, her money would go to her food or tobacco addiction instead of paying her rent. "Diddy, without you, I'd be outta my money in a week," she's often said.

Still, about once a month she sweet-talks me into a ten spot for snuff. "Better make it a twenty, 'cuz I need my dia-pers," is a sentence that I never thought would light me up with joy, but it did when Vanessa, once so shy about her health problems, recently shouted it across a large room. She is no longer ashamed. She rarely says thank you but beams with bright wattage. Today, Vanessa is back in her own apart-ment, a few miles from our campus at a building where the apartment manager accepts tenants at a reduced rate as long as we provide ongoing case management and commit to walk beside them.

Most folks would observe a week in Vanessa's life and de-termine that she is a drain on resources and a liability to our success story. To the contrary, I would respond that Vanessa is no longer living in squalor and at risk of abuse in the streets. After twenty years of solitude, she now has a family that loves her, takes care of her on her birthday and at Christ-mas, hugs her even when she reeks of snuff and urine, and tells her she looks pretty on those rare occasions when she dresses up for an event. I'd respond that Vanessa has been as much transformed as anyone.

Early on, Rhonda counseled me to accept that many folks who would come our way would be ours to provide care to for the rest of their life, or the rest of ours, whichever came first. For so long I saw that as accepting failure. Now I understand it as investing in dignity. We will never break poverty's cycle if there are people who we're willing to leave behind. When someone says, "We can't take care of everyone!" they probably are pretty confident they will never be *everyone*. They're also apt to believe that hard luck is in fact always earned. The real truth is that Rufus and Vanessa and so many others like them never got their shot to spin the wheel. They were left behind, as were their parents before them. We help them because it's the right thing to do but also because it's the only way to stop the cycle. Vanessa will never know the child who was taken from her when she was twelve, but the son raised by his father's family now has a relationship with her. He'll never have to tell anyone again that his mother is homeless or worry that she's on the streets.

ONE OF THE GREAT JOYS and accomplishments of City of Refuge is in showing people that they can do so much more than others think they can. Getting people to trust in that belief requires them to reject all those labels society has stamped on them—and with them, the binary, time-bound "success-failure" mind-set that troubles me when it comes to measuring our impact.

I myself love being able to do more than others think I can. Three or four times a week, I finish the day in our campus weight room, where my daughters put in several miles on the treadmill and a couple of my staff and I lift weights. Each week my son-in-law, Matt, prints out workout plans that increase in intensity over the course of each ten-week plan. At fifty-seven, I am proud to say that I hold my own in those workouts. Long ago the younger staff members stopped accepting the challenge to compete with me to see who could bench-press the most weight. I will admit, I get a euphoric rush when I see a staff member or guest look at the amount of weight on the bar, look at me, and shake their heads, doubting my ability to succeed.

One day the weight goal for me was more than I had achieved at any point in the past. My son-in-law assured me the amount listed on my workout plan was correct and that he was sure I could lift it. After several warm-up sets, I took my place on the bench and lifted the bar down off the supports. About halfway up I began to struggle as the bar started a slow descent toward my chest. Matt was spotting me and quickly grabbed the middle of the bar. Together we lifted it and placed it in the supports.

"First time I've ever seen you fail," said Matt with a bit of astonishment in his voice. I'm still amazed today that he fully expected I was going to be successful at the highest weight I had ever attempted to lift. At the same time, *fail* is not a word I like to hear tossed in my direction. My first impulse was to check and see who saw. Moments later, I instructed Matt to reload the bar at the same weight. Lying down on the bench, I cleared my mind of my last attempt. I would start clean, with no reason to expect anything but success. I inhaled deeply and pushed the bar as high as my arms would reach, drawing deeply from my reserves. Just like that, I successfully completed the bench-press with the same amount of weight I had failed with moments before. Inside, I was shouting in victory and dancing a celebration, but to Matt I just gave a broad smile.

MATT HAD BEEN QUICK to draw a conclusion in his mental "impact report." But what Matt didn't understand was that in my own mind, I hadn't failed at all—I just wasn't finished yet. This, in a nutshell, is the attitude that has kept me going through all these years of offering second, third, and thirtieth chances. I've replaced that limiting success-failure binary with the deep recognition that every one of us is in a lifelong journey of becoming. If someone stumbles or doubts the trust

I have in them, I haven't failed and neither have they. We just haven't finished yet.

For example, Victoria Hope (formerly Stephanie) is, like me and like you, still on her journey. The time at the ranch was wonderful; she was more content and in control than we'd ever seen her. This lasted for a couple months, then the demons of yesteryear revisited and crisis management was required again. That cycle repeated itself a number of times and intervention was required. Our clinicians and staff heatedly debated the best approach to support her. Fatigue and doubt set in on more than one occasion. But, just as my father had believed in me, I chose to believe in Victoria. Because my father, even in the final hours of his pain, remained intent on expressing his belief in me, I had the strength to tell Victoria I believed in her. Because finishing well was modeled for me, the decision to continue the journey with Victoria was an easy one to make even in the midst of the struggle. Trust and time, time and trust.

I CAN'T RESIST another sports analogy; as my daughters readily will tell you, I believe there's a lot of wisdom to be taken from team sports and the discipline of physical fitness. At our weekly basketball games, I'm once again typically the oldest guy on the court. I always choose to cover someone who is my peer in speed and skill. Long ago I stopped letting my ego match myself with someone thirty years my junior who runs faster and jumps higher than I do. I finally realized that being the best is not what should drive me. Using the knowledge, skill, and experience I have to contribute to my team's success is far more important and rewarding than having the highest number of points or standing out in the game.

We generally play a minimum of four full-court games each Wednesday evening, sometimes five or six. I pace myself, knowing that going all out in game one will guarantee I am nearly useless in game four. My good sense means I usually have more left in the tank at the end than the young bucks on either my team or the opposing one. Doing good work well requires stamina and strategy, underwritten by the recognition that your journey of becoming is just that— *yours*. It's up to each of us to define success by parameters that are meaningful and attainable and to pursue the goals that bring us dignity and joy so that we can keep contributing in whatever way we are capable. The more we can do this for ourselves, the more capable we will be in helping others to master the same pursuit.

When it comes to City of Refuge, we have a clear plan for the future. We'll keep writing those impact reports. But the truth is there is no end goal. Transformation requires an eternal outlook. We'll faithfully count the beds slept in, the meals eaten, the women rescued, but meanwhile we will measure our own success according to one question, asked again and again, in perpetuity: How do I do good better today than I did yesterday?

Victoria stopped by my office not long ago and showed me the grades she had just received from the college where she is enrolled—four Bs and an A. We talked a bit about the car we had given her and the new tires our auto shop had placed on it just that morning. A few minutes of general conversation passed, and wrapping up our time together, Victoria asked, "Pastor Bruce, can I have a hug?" It might surprise you to hear that I'm not a natural hugger. My wife doles out most of the hugs. But Victoria's radiant joy and desire to share it with an embrace transformed me in that moment. Without even a trace of apprehension, I gave her a hug, kissed her on the cheek, and told her I loved her. She smiled shyly, said goodbye, and headed out.

I don't have the capability or the desire to guess who among those who come to me in need will eventually be in a position to serve someone else. I can't do the math on it, but my experience tells me that our best hope in recasting someone's future—in breaking a cycle so oppressive it seems predestined—lies in offering a trusting and faithful heart, again and again if necessary, until a person is ready to accept it. Then you only have to be willing to walk together, as long as it takes.

CHAPTER 12

The Next Thing

Be thou the rainbow over the storms of life!
The evening beam that smiles the clouds away,
and tints to-morrow with prophetic ray.

—LORD BYRON, *The Bride of Abydos*

Twenty-one years is a long time. You might think being in an environment of ongoing crisis, hardship, and urgency of need would make that time seem even longer. That's not at all the case. Twenty-one years have passed in a blur, but I only have to look at my now-grown daughters to be jolted into the reality of now. Three of them work and serve at City of Refuge, one is school teacher, and the youngest is a high school junior who loves living here on campus, where we once again have a home, thanks to local zoning changes. In one average trip from my office to the cafeteria, I'm inevitably stopped to shake four or five hands, be they people in our programs, employees, volunteers, or donors, and weigh in on two or three problems. When I stop to notice, the evidence that we've been at this for two decades and counting is all around us.

Meanwhile, much has changed in the 30314 vicinity, particularly in the past handful of years. The neighborhood is now in the shadow of a shiny new sports arena, the $1.5 billion Mercedes-Benz Stadium, opened in 2017, just over a mile down the road from our warehouse. Its owner, Arthur M. Blank, a cofounder of Home Depot, has put $20 million toward his promise that this stadium, unlike the two previous ones in downtown Atlanta, will improve quality of life for its distressed neighbors. Blank's foundation has made some great investments in the neighborhood—among them new parks and a jobs program similar to our own. But not too surprisingly, many locals have been hesitant to trust whether he and others with ambitious "revitalization plans" have their best interests at heart. I've heard people say they see a lot more talking then listening.

Real estate speculators are still sitting on hundreds of vacant, dilapidated properties, and rents are on the rise. There are plans for a couple of huge developments in Vine City and English Avenue (our two adjacent neighborhoods) that would create hundreds of new affordable rentals, but they're probably years down the pike. On the positive side, police data in 2018 showed that crime was down 40 percent in those same neighborhoods, after a three-year federal crackdown on open-air drug markets, a game of enforcement whack-a-mole. More hopeful is the work of the mayor of Atlanta, Keisha Lance Bottoms, who is from the Westside and who I've heard call it "her heart." She has focused her administration on education, criminal justice reform, and affordable housing, including property tax subsidies for homeowners in the Westside at risk of displacement. The city, in cooperation with multiple non-profits, has spent and earmarked many millions of dollars for Westside economic and community development. And while City of Refuge lies just outside their immediate geographic target (and we don't pursue public funding, anyway), we're excited by the momentum we see, as are many locals, especially older folks who can still recall a better, safer time in the neighborhood they still call home.

There are also those days where it seems we've made no progress at all. August 12, 2018, was a recent one. Beverly Jenkins, one of our most beloved staff members, left our campus when her shift ended at midnight, and was killed at a gas station a mile away. She was a grandmother helping raise three grandkids. Some young men tried to rob her, got spooked, and shot her dead. The story barely even made the news. On our campus, staff and residents gathered in circles in our parking lot for two days, weeping and comforting one another; her absence will be painful for much, much longer than that. Four staff members quit after her death, saying they didn't feel safe coming to work anymore. Others became more committed than ever.

The outpouring of grief after her death reminded me that the work our staff and volunteers do, at all hours of the day and night, is about so much more than the provision of resources. They are each making irreplaceable gifts of the soul. Horticulture was one of Beverly's passions, and she taught so many residents the joy of nurturing and growing plants. Many walls in Eden Village were galleries for her paintings. The only consolation, a very small one, was that City of Refuge had the network and resources to immediately shower her family with financial and emotional support. They know beyond doubt how much their mother Beverly meant to her community.

DARK DAYS DO ARRIVE, but we keep waking up each day looking for ways to do good better. Finding safe, comfortable, and affordable housing for our employees and for people who graduate from our programs is increasingly difficult. With this in mind, we embarked on an initiative to build apartments and single-family dwellings to house those in our vocational-training programs, graduates of our residential programs, and residents in the community looking for safe and affordable housing that includes support services. We purchased an old, decrepit apartment building across the street from our property along with a number of lots and abandoned homes in the community around us. We are cleaning up overgrown lots and removing truckloads of trash. In October 2018, we broke ground on a forty-seven-unit apartment complex, our first major expansion beyond the warehouse. We've decided not to fence in the property. There will be night security guards, but otherwise, we'll trust the tenants themselves to maintain the safe space. Everyone who signs a lease will also agree to be an active participant in community meetings and property maintenance. And just as we do with our staff, we'll lay down the cultural basics—love, acceptance, and a non-judgmental attitude. Everything else will be up to them.

As we replace these former havens for violent crime with safe spaces, one by one, we are hoping that over time, the effect will ripple out into the neighborhood, where we continue to build ties of community. We are having dinners with long-time residents in our community and asking for their recollections of the past and their dreams for the future. Together we are envisioning a neighborhood where residents feel safe again to sit in the cool of the evening, reflecting and sharing stories about life, family, and sports. A neighborhood where children graduate from elementary to middle to high school and eventually have the opportunity for secondary education or a chance to enter the workforce with a living-wage income. A neighborhood where City of Refuge no longer needs a guard booth and its own eight-foot fence, and I don't need to worry that employees won't make it back home to the arms of their grandchildren.

————————

HAVING WHAT OTHERS DEEM as success in this space means I am now asked to tell our story around the country on a regular basis. People from multiple cities and communities have reached out and inquired about City of Refuge establishing a site in their neighborhood. We have done that in a number of places but have had to decline those invitations many more times than we have been able to say yes. We now have affiliates in more than ten cities, including Chicago, Baltimore, and Dallas.

There has been a good bit of recognition of our work, and accolades and awards have come along now and again— worth mentioning if only because it contrasts so completely with all those years of being told I was nuts. Many churches and nonprofits want to learn from our one-stop-shop, collective-impact model and want me to help them find their way as they work to empower and impact others. I guess these are good things, as they help us promote our work and raise money, so we can do more ourselves all while helping other folks do good well. We want to be a place where people can come to be inspired and then return home ready to tackle the challenges of their own communities.

Truthfully, the stuff that takes me off campus, away from our large and growing community, wearies me. Some have counseled me that this phase of life is the "next thing" and that I should embrace the chance to stand on the stage, be the focus of the story, have my name listed as an expert in my field. I see the opportunity it presents for our work, so I'm there—but on a personal level, I really just want the "next thing" to be more of the same thing I have been privileged to do for the past two decades.

Twenty-one years is a long time, and it is no time. It has taken every one of those years for us to develop relationships, carve out a strategy, and execute on an ever-evolving plan. Much like an athlete who has trained for years and finally gets in the game, we at City of Refuge feel as though our time is now arriving. The chance to do more than we ever thought possible is right in front of us, and we are moving from the introduction of the story of our journey to chapter 1. We can't wait to see how the script unfolds.

THERE ARE A MULTITUDE of Rufuses and Glorias in our cities, and they, at some point, will need someone to step into their conflict and, with heart racing and sweat pouring, convince them that life is more than what they see today and hope is greater than the rage they are currently experiencing. Jake leans against the utility pole in communities around the world, too proud to ask for help, let alone love, but desperately in need of both. He's waiting for someone to cross the street, shake his hand, and simply share their name. People like our Vanessa and Stephanie and Ryan call your city and community home but don't believe they are valuable. No one has yet spoken that value into their souls. Sons and daughters who are homeless, addicted, convicted, alone, and without hope are waiting for someone to bring them home.

I mentioned earlier that most of the "lifers" in the City of Refuge volunteer community didn't come to us already on a mission to help those less fortunate. Many came simply because they were curious. Some didn't want to come at all—for example, Doug. When his wife told him she was going to visit our campus, he tried to convince her not to go—the neighborhood was way too dangerous, he said. Why would she want to put herself at risk? When she told him she was going to visit anyway, he finally agreed to go with her, rather than let her go alone. On campus, he met our staff, and the people in our programs, and got to know the work we were doing. On that first visit, his heart shifted in a fundamental way. Today, eight years later, he is a long-standing member of our board of directors, using his business management background to help us create the processes that give our residents the best possible experience. And needless to say, his relationship with our neighborhood is transformed. Any sense of "them" has been replaced with "us."

Deep in all of us resides a trusting, compassionate spirit, and we all want others to experience opportunities that will allow them to live in places of peace and self-fulfillment. We all have more than the mere capability to approach others in a spirit of trust—we have the *need*. To trust and be trusted is among our deepest human urges. Life without deep community is anxious and unsatisfying, leaving an emptiness that no purchase or accomplishment can fill. I personally have found that there's nothing more satisfying than putting another person's needs before your own.

Taking more risks of trust and compassion doesn't require you to move into a busted-up church or start your own nonprofit. My younger brother, Keith, and his family have friends of their children from difficult home environments living with them, and they invest resources and talent into others daily. April, my sister, was the primary caregiver for her father-in-law as he endured the ravages of brain cancer, and she cared for our dying father and now our mother. True, their stories may not contain risk to life and limb or uprooting their lives to help strangers, but their stories, and many of yours, contain incredible examples of light, hope, and transformation. Every one of those stories is equally valuable.

There is still much work to do, many people to meet, dreams to help become reality. Together with volunteers, staff, donors, and friends from various walks of life, we will change our community. As you will change yours.

You'll have to excuse me now. I just got a message that Harold, aka Roy, aka Jamaica, is threatening to kill Jeff in the dining hall. Send thoughts and prayers my way if you would. I'll let you know how it goes.

Acknowledgments

My life would not be complete and this book would not have been possible without the love and support shared freely with me over the past thirty-two years by my incredible wife, Rhonda; she is definitely Beauty to her Beast. The gifts known as Kassi, Kelsi, Kensi, Kaylin, and Karli, our five beautiful daughters, are more than I ever dreamed I would receive. They have now added sons-in-law Matt, Garrison, and Andrew to the dinner table, and Kade, Kase, and Asher are deeply loved by this Papa.

My dad and mom, Cecil and Dawn Deel, never wavered in their love for God, their family, and those in need. They shared that spirit of commitment with me, and I am the man I am today as a result of their influence and example.

My brother Jeff has been alongside for this extended, slow walk of obedience for twenty-one of the twenty-two years, and his steadiness has served City of Refuge and me well.

My younger siblings, Keith and April, are far more than just family; they are friends in the best kind of way.

I have more extended family than can be counted and certainly too many to list here, but they helped to shape and form me and truly revealed the power of a tribe caring for one of its own.

Hundreds of staff persons have served the organization and me personally by sharing their time, talents, and treasure with great generosity. The good we have been able to do is directly attributable to those men and women.

Over the past years thousands of individuals have been a part of the City of Refuge story of light, hope, and transformation. Together as donors, volunteers, tutors, mentors, and friends they have paved the rough roads, leveled the highest hills, bridged the troubled waters, and labored beside me in both success and failure. I am truly grateful for each of those whose path has crossed with mine

Sara Grace took my big dream and helped refine it into a story that simply feels right. Her passion and heartfelt energy for the project made working with a cowriter a real joy.

Editor extraordinaire Leah Trouwborst and the publicity and marketing team at Portfolio/Penguin Random House provided incredibly valuable insight and wisdom to this first-time author, and I am better for having worked with each of them. Adrian Zackheim challenged me to think bigger and write better, and I am indebted.

Simon Sinek first encouraged me to put our story on paper, and he has walked with me from day one. His knowledge and experience were shared freely with me, and I do not have the words to express my level of gratitude. Sara Toborowsky, with Start with Why, and Jay Mandel, with WEM, also jumped in my boat and helped me row in the right direction.

I am grateful to Rufus, Gloria, Jake, Vanessa, Ryan, Greg, Tennie, and a multitude of others who accepted the trust we offered and chose to extend the same trust back. Not all the stories ended as we wished but I would not have missed a single one. Each was a gift in its own way.

Finally, to God the Father, creator of heaven and earth, be all glory and honor and power and thanksgiving. Amen.